ZEN x LEADERSHIP

THE ART OF SYNERGIZING PARADOXES

SHARADA ATTILI

Made with ♥ on the Notion Press Platform
www.notionpress.com

ॐ श्री गुरुभ्यो नमः

For all of you who have illuminated my path
with your wisdom, this book is a tribute to the
lessons you have imparted.

Contents

Acknowledgements

This book is a vessel, shaped by many hands, just as my life has been and will continue to be.

Thank you Dr Mani Pavitra. Your are the trigger and catalyst for this book. Had it not been your entry into my life, this story would not have taken shape and literal form. I will forever be indebted for the *sreekaaram* of my authoring journey.

Thank you to the dynamic and resilient real-life Vikram - the one who is and the one who could have been. You led me to explore the art of leadership—a journey as personal to me as it is universal.

Thank you Amruta for being the in-house proofreader and artist who brought my mental image to life.

Dear Reader, thank you for embarking on this journey with me. The story you hold in your hand has shaped me and your presence turns these pages from mere words to living wisdom. May they echo your own leadership quest and inspire bold steps ahead.

Preface

In the grand tapestry of human existence, paradoxes are the threads that weave together the fabric of our lives. These enigmatic juxtapositions of opposites challenge our understanding, forcing us to navigate the complex interplay of light and shadow, strength and vulnerability, ambition and humility. Within the world of leadership, these paradoxes are not mere philosophical conundrums; they are the very essence of transformative growth.They embody serene wisdom alongside vibrant vitality of generations of leaders, crafting an approach that is both timeless and immediate

Vikram Sharma's Journey

Our story begins with Vikram Sharma, an experienced and dedicated leader in the bustling expanse of business. Vikram, like many of us, had embarked on his leadership journey with a vision—a vision of growth, innovation, and making a meaningful impact. As a steward of development, Vikram has been instrumental in propelling his enterprises toward significant transformation.

Yet, his journey is marked by the ebb and flow of triumph and tribulation, embodying the ZenX spirit of leadership. His path mirrors the intricate balance of two steps forward, occasionally a step backward, a perpetual spiral where progress is punctuated with moments of contemplation — a dance of advancing

PREFACE

while embracing the wisdom of stepping back, all in the pursuit of enduring change.

The SOAR Approach

In his journey, Vikram uncovered the truth that growth is not a linear process. It's not a straightforward path but a delicate dance—a dance that finds beauty in life's contradictions. This insight crystallized into the SOAR approach:

SOAR

S

Self-Reflect

Look at where you're stuck and figure out how to get better.

O

Own Your Journey

Know that falling down is part of getting better. Make clear plans and follow them step by step.

A

Act With Persistence

Don't stop moving forward. Use your mistakes as lessons and stick to your goals.

R

Rise Higher

Be proud of what you achieve, share what you learn, and aim ever upwards.

PREFACE

The Essence of Leadership Paradox

At the heart of "ZenX Leadership: The Art of Synergizing Paradoxes" lies the acceptance that leadership is an exploration of balancing contrasts. It is not simply a role played but a dynamic journey through the intersecting forces of steadfastness and adaptability, ambition and understanding, decisiveness and openness.

This approach to leadership doesn't see paradoxes as hurdles but as opportunities for growth and creative solutions. It's about combining the forward thrust of ambition with the gentleness of empathy, the clarity of decisive action with the wisdom of open-mindedness, and the foresight of vision with the grounding of humility.

In this dance of dichotomies, leaders flourish. They navigate the complexities of today's ever-evolving world by synergizing these paradoxes, crafting an approach that is both centered and expansive, reflective of the ZenX essence—leading not by choosing between opposing forces but by blending them into a cohesive, powerful whole.

Strength and Vulnerability:
A great leader must be strong and resilient, able to weather storms and make tough decisions. Yet, true strength lies not in an impenetrable facade but in the vulnerability to admit mistakes, learn from failures, and connect with others on a human level. It's the delicate balance of being unyielding when necessary and open-

hearted when needed that distinguishes exceptional leaders.

Ambition and Empathy:
Ambition is the driving force behind progress and achievement. It propels leaders to set audacious goals and inspire their teams to reach new heights. However, empathy steers ambition by reminding us that no one person has all the answers. Effective leaders understand that acknowledging their limitations and valuing the contributions of others are not signs of weakness but hallmarks of wisdom.

Decisiveness and Open-mindedness:
Leaders are often called upon to make critical decisions swiftly and decisively. Yet, the best decisions emerge from a fertile ground of open-mindedness. The ability to consider diverse perspectives, question assumptions, and adapt to changing circumstances is what separates leaders who merely manage crises from those who lead transformative change.

Vision and Humility:
Visionaries see possibilities where others see obstacles. They chart ambitious courses for their organizations, inspiring others to follow. However, humility tempers vision by grounding it in reality. Humble leaders understand that their vision is not infallible and that success is the result of collective effort. They are open to course corrections and embrace feedback as a means of refining their vision.

Leaders who embrace these paradoxes do more than merely lead; they thrive in the complex landscape of the modern world. They understand that leadership is not about choosing one quality over another but about mastering the art of balance.

Prologue

The Paradox of Leadership

At the heart of this book lies a concept as multifaceted as it is powerful—Synergizing the paradoxes within leadership. This concept is the cornerstone of our journey, and it's essential to understand the mosaic it creates by blending elements of fiction, management lessons, and self-help wisdom.

The Intersection of Fiction

Fiction, in its myriad forms, has always been a mirror that reflects the human condition. It allows us to step into the shoes of characters, to experience their joys and tribulations, and to witness the consequences of their choices. In this book, fiction serves as our narrative vessel—a medium that brings abstract leadership concepts to life through the experiences of relatable characters.

Through the lens of fiction, we gain a deeper understanding of leadership by immersing ourselves in the challenges, dilemmas, and triumphs of our protagonist, Vikram. His journey is a mirror that reflects the leadership journey we all undertake in our own lives, albeit with different contexts and challenges.

PROLOGUE

The Wisdom of Management Lessons

Management lessons are the wellspring of practical knowledge, honed in the crucible of real-world experiences. They offer actionable insights into the art and science of leadership. In this book, these lessons are interwoven seamlessly with the narrative, allowing us to extract wisdom from the characters' experiences.

As we accompany Vikram on his leadership odyssey, we will pause to dissect key management principles that emerge organically from the narrative. These lessons serve as guiding lights, illuminating the path to effective leadership, and highlighting the importance of strategic thinking, team dynamics, and decision-making.

The Insights of Self-Help Wisdom

Self-help wisdom is the foundation upon which personal growth is built. It offers tools and techniques to navigate life's complexities, foster self-awareness, and harness one's full potential. This book incorporates self-help wisdom to provide you, the reader, with actionable strategies for your own personal and leadership development.

Within these pages, you'll discover practical exercises, reflective prompts, and self-assessment tools that bridge the gap between theory and practice. They empower you to apply the lessons learned from the characters' experiences to your own life, fostering self-awareness, resilience, and a sense of purpose.

PROLOGUE

"ZenX Leadership:

The Art of Synergizing Paradoxes" is more than just a concept; it's a living, breathing narrative that fuses the power of fiction, the wisdom of management lessons, and the insights of self-help guidance. It invites you to embark on a journey where theory and practice converge, where characters' stories become mirrors reflecting your own leadership path.

As we traverse this paradoxical terrain, remember that leadership is not a destination but a continuous exploration—a journey of self-discovery, growth, and transformation. It is our hope that the synergy of these elements will illuminate your path, enrich your understanding of leadership, and empower you to become a more effective, empathetic, and resilient leader in all aspects of your life.

Welcome to ZenX Leadership: The Art of Synergizing Paradoxes, where the convergence of fiction, management lessons, and self-help wisdom paves the way for transformative growth.

Who Is This Book For?

Before we embark on this transformative journey through the world of leadership and paradox, it's essential to clarify who this book is for and why it matters to a diverse array of readers.

This book is primarily crafted for those who aspire to lead, whether in the realms of business, community, or personal life. It's for the emerging leaders who sense that leadership is not merely about authority but about a deeper understanding of self and others. If you're a manager looking to elevate your leadership skills, this book is your compass. In the modern professional landscape, the line between management and leadership is increasingly blurred. Understanding the paradoxes of leadership is essential for effective management. This book offers valuable insights to help you evolve from a manager into a leader.

Moreover, leadership is not confined to boardrooms and offices. It's a concept that resonates with anyone on a personal journey of growth and self-discovery. Whether you're someone seeking to unlock your hidden potential, to navigate the complexities of life's decisions, or to better understand the leadership roles you play in your own life, this book is a guiding light.

Leadership is a subject that transcends industries and professions. If you're a lifelong learner, an inquisitive mind hungry for knowledge and personal development, you'll find this book to be a wellspring of wisdom. It offers a unique perspective on leadership that blends management principles with the art of living a purposeful life.

Paradoxes are the mysteries that fuel our intellectual curiosity. If you're someone who finds joy in unraveling the complexities of life's paradoxes, this book is a treasure trove. It delves into the enigmatic interplay of opposing forces, inviting you to explore the beauty and wisdom hidden within the paradoxes of leadership.

Whether you're an aspiring leader, a seasoned manager, a seeker of self-discovery, a lifelong learner, or simply a curious mind, this book is designed with you in mind. The paradoxes of leadership are universal, and their exploration transcends boundaries. We invite you to embark on this journey with an open heart and a thirst for wisdom, for within these pages, you will discover the transformative power of leadership and paradox.

The Awakening

CHAPTER 1

The Call of Leadership

The year was 1980. Vikram stands at the crossroads of his life in the vibrant streets of Mumbai, and his journey, like many great tales, is about to unfold.

Vikram is embarking on his first day at the bank, a place of financial transactions and calculative precision. It's a path well-trodden by his family – his father retired from this very institution just a year ago, and his elder brother started his career here three years prior. The bank is more than a workplace; it's a family legacy, a torch passed from one generation to the next.

The corridors of the bank resonate with stories of his father's wisdom and dedication, tales of the lives he touched, and the respect he earned. It's a legacy that has imprinted itself upon Vikram's heart since childhood. He has witnessed the impact his father had on people, no matter where his career took him, be it small villages or bustling cities. In the eyes of those he served, his father was more than a banker; he was a ray of hope and financial wisdom.

As Vikram makes his way to his first day at the bank, memories of bedtime tales whispered by his maternal grandparents flood his thoughts. Their stories aren't mundane bedtime fables but narratives of valor and sacrifice. They fought for India's freedom, marching against the British, enduring lathi blows, and years in the confines of jails alongside fellow freedom fighters. Decades have passed since the country gained independence, yet the flame of patriotism still burns brightly within them. Their unwavering call to duty, even in their twilight years, echoes deeply within Vikram. They are living reminders of the struggles and sacrifices made to shape the future of his generation. Their voices play in his mind, urging him to contribute his part to building the nation, to make a difference in the lives of those he will encounter.

Vikram has bigger shoes to fill, and these memories serve as the bedrock of his unwavering dedication and sense of purpose. The indomitable spirit of his grandparents becomes the driving force behind his commitment to not only follow a path of success but to use that success as a means to uplift people. Their legacy infuses him with a sense of duty and objectivity, shaping him into a resolute and purpose-driven individual ready to embark on a journey of impact and transformation.

With these thoughts swirling in his mind, Vikram embarks on his journey into the world of banking, armed with a burning desire to create an impact and serve a higher purpose. He knows that every great leader, including his father and grandparents, has been fueled by a similar fiery determination. It's this inner flame that powers their actions, a source of inexhaustible energy and unwavering drive.

As he steps into the bank, Vikram is aware that his position is temporary, a placeholder for an employee on long leave. His brother advises him to make the most of it and is determined. He has limited time to prove his mettle and show them he can be a great asset to the bank. Exactly as he has decided, within a few months, he earns himself an offer for a permanent position. His exceptional performance becomes a talking point across the departments and becomes a testament to his dedication and competence. His family rejoices at this milestone, but surprisingly not Vikram. He has been feeling a growing sense of unease for some time.

You see, Vikram's initial steps into the world of banking bring with them a mixture of emotions. While he holds deep respect for the institution and understands its significance, he cannot escape the feeling of disconnection with the daily routines of his job. Although he proves to be a quick learner, excelling in his tasks with remarkable efficiency, Vikram finds himself in constant introspection. The bank, once a place of reverence and promise, has slowly become a drudgery which he has not expected. What he sees around definitely does not quite align with his inner aspirations. Despite the seemingly well-paved and secure path ahead, something within him yearns for a different adventure and a deeper sense of purpose.

This nagging feeling gradually develops over time when slowly a unique gift becomes self-evident. He possesses the uncanny ability to connect with people on a profound level. He spends hours engaging in conversations with those who visit the bank, listening intently to their dreams, plans, and ambitions. These interactions fuel his spirit, and he relishes the opportunity to understand people's aspirations. Hours slip away as he engages in conversations, listening intently to people, especially those seeking business loans. It's in his interactions with the people who visit the bank that Vikram discovers a connection. He is drawn to their dreams, their plans, and their unwavering ambition.

When the moment arrives to sign the papers that will confirm his permanent role at the bank, Vikram's pen hesitates, as if suspended in time. His mind is filled with thoughts of an offer that has come unexpectedly the previous evening, an offer that tugs at the very fabric of his existence.

The evening before had been unlike any other in Vikram's life. It was an evening that would alter the course of his journey in ways he couldn't yet fathom. Rajan Verma, one of the relatively older lot in his neighborhood, pulls him aside with an offer that echoes in his mind like a tantalizing whisper. Over the months of working, Vikram develops a routine of spending each evening hanging out with friends and neighbors in the colony park. It's an ingrained routine - wash up after going home, snack on whatever his mother lays out, and head out to the park next lane. Through all the goofing around, it turns out Vikram makes quite an impression on Rajan. Rajan Verma has recently returned from Delhi, bringing with him stories of a life different from anything Vikram has known. What fascinates Vikram even more are Rajan's tales of attempting to establish his own manufacturing firm in the capital. Over endless cups of tea, both of them have developed a brotherly bond and camaraderie. Rajan shares the struggles, the setbacks, and the relentless pursuit of a dream that defines his existence.

The offer Rajan extends the previous evening is a proposition for partnership in the very manufacturing venture that has featured in his dreams. Rajan has been searching for a partner who possesses the same passion and boundless energy that he has found in Vikram. Their unique blend of technical expertise and the ability to connect with people makes them the ideal team. Throughout the night, Vikram wrestles with his conflicting emotions. In his mind's eye, he sees two distinct paths unfolding before him—a path where he will follow in his father's footsteps as a banker, and another, where he will venture into the unknown as a businessman, shaping his legacy. None in his life has ever tried any kind of business ever.

As Vikram stands in the General Manager's cabin, pen poised over the papers, he can't bring himself to sign them. The offer from Rajan is tinged with the promise of a different path, drowning out the familiar security of a banking career. Vikram's heart resonates with the truth. He knows that his true calling lies in embracing the role of an adventurer, a visionary, and a leader. It's a decision that will change the trajectory of his life, setting him on a course filled with uncertainty and boundless potential.

That is the moment he walks out of the bank. His GM sees the struggle and encourages him on his chosen path. He sees what Vikram is made of and knows his decision is the right one. With a few words of advice, he bids farewell to Vikram.

As the next morning sun paints the city's skyline with hues of hope and possibility, Vikram embarks on a journey that will eventually lead to the birth of DynaGrow Ventures. The decision to step into the realm of entrepreneurship marks the beginning of a new chapter, one where he will harness his inner visionary and pioneer a path less traveled.

The call of leadership has beckoned, and Vikram has answered with unwavering determination. In the days that follow, he will face challenges, make sacrifices, and navigate uncharted territories, all in pursuit of his vision. DynaGrow Ventures will take its first breath, and the world will soon witness the transformative journey of a visionary leader.

It will take time to temper the high emotions of his decision within his family. Convincing his father, earning his brother's understanding, and establishing DynaGrow as an equal partnership with Rajan will require both patience and perseverance. But for Vikram, the challenges are a part of the journey, milestones on the path to realizing his vision.

With determination burning in his heart, Vikram knows that the next step is to secure the capital needed to breathe life into their entrepreneurial dream. He turns to his father, a man of wisdom and experience, for guidance and support.

Vikram's father, recognizing his son's unwavering resolve and commitment, offers a solution that will set the wheels of their entrepreneurial journey in motion. He suggests selling a piece of farmland in their ancestral village, a piece of land that holds sentimental value but is no longer of practical use to the family.

Vikram is entrusted with the task of selling the farmland, with an expected figure in mind. His father, known for his pragmatism, sets a challenge before Vikram. If he can sell the land for a figure exceeding the expected amount, he will be allowed to retain the difference as his earning - the capital for DynaGrow Ventures.

Vikram embraces this challenge with zeal, and within a mere month, he not only matches Rajan's investment but exceeds it. With the capital secured, DynaGrow Ventures is born as an equal partnership between Vikram and Rajan, each bringing their unique strengths and aspirations to the table. The dream team sets forth on a path their capabilities are destined for, a path their courage paves for them.

Avoiding Missed Opportunities: A SOAR Perspective

As we immerse ourselves in Vikram's journey at the crossroads of security and adventure, it provides us with an opportunity to explore essential leadership principles applicable to our own paths. Leadership often leads us to pivotal moments of decision, where we must grapple with paradoxes and make choices that shape our trajectory. Vikram's story serves as a mirror, reflecting the complexities and opportunities inherent in leadership.

Consider for a moment the opportunities you may have missed due to hesitation or a fear of change. How often have you continued down a familiar path simply because you had invested significant time and effort in it, even when doubts crept into your choices? Vikram's resolute action in embracing entrepreneurship challenges us to reflect on our own decisions.

Let's navigate these concepts through the SOAR model, offering straightforward steps that you can integrate into your daily leadership journey:

S - Self-Reflection:

Take a pause to assess your current position in your leadership journey. Are you on a path that genuinely resonates with your ambitions and values, or have you been following a trajectory out of familiarity or comfort? Vikram's introspective moment underscores the importance of understanding our inner callings.

O - Own Your Journey:

Recognize that setbacks and doubts are natural aspects of growth. Summon the courage to take ownership of your decisions, even if it entails deviating from a well-trodden path. Vikram's bold choice to embrace entrepreneurship exemplifies this principle.

A - Act with Persistence:

Vikram's determination to persistently pursue his vision despite uncertainties serves as an inspiration. When faced with adversity or doubt, remember that persistence is the key to moving forward. Learn from your mistakes, adapt to challenges, and remain committed to your goals.

R - Rise Higher:

Celebrate those moments when you choose to rise above convention and embrace your inner visionary. Understand that success is not solely defined by conventional achievements but also by your personal growth and impact. Use Vikram's journey as a reminder to continually strive for new heights in your leadership path.

SOAR
S
Self-Reflect
Pause and assess your leadership path
O
Own Your Journey
Embrace setbacks as part of growth.
A
Act With Persistence
Persist in pursuit of your vision.
R
Rise Higher
Celebrate your moments of leadership success

Incorporating these straightforward principles into your life can help you navigate the complexities of leadership with clarity and purpose. Vikram's story invites us to reflect on our own choices, recognize our strengths and weaknesses, and act decisively when faced with the paradoxes between security and ambition. It's a call to avoid missed opportunities and make choices that align with our true leadership potential.

It will take time for the dust to settle around his decision, but Vikram remains resolutely focused on the path he has chosen. Convincing his father, earning his brother's understanding, and establishing DynaGrow as an equal partnership with Rajan will require both patience and perseverance. Yet, for Vikram, these challenges are an integral part of his journey, marking significant milestones on the path to realizing his vision.

CHAPTER 2

Expanding Horizons

The journey of Vikram Sharma and Rajan with DynaGrow Ventures was at its nascent stage, marked by the thrilling decision to embrace entrepreneurship. This momentous step had thrust them into the exhilarating yet unpredictable world of business, where the 1980s and early 1990s ushered in a wave of economic reforms in India, opening doors to both opportunities and challenges.

Their entrepreneurial odyssey kicks off with a paradox that will define their path: Strength versus Vulnerability. Vikram possesses a unique strength in his ability to connect with people, deciphering their needs and dreams. On the other hand, Rajan stands as the technical cornerstone of their partnership, armed with unmatched expertise in the technology and his knowledge of manufacturing processes. Together, they are a force to be reckoned with, yet they soon come to realize that their journey will be rife with unexpected turns.

The initial years are a crucible of relentless learning and tireless effort. They delve into the complexities of manufacturing, supply chains, and the intricate web of customer relationships. Each obstacle they encounter becomes an opportunity to test their mettle and adaptability. Vikram's remarkable capacity to embrace vulnerability becomes his secret weapon; he isn't afraid to admit when he lacks answers, seeking guidance from Rajan and other industry experts.

A formidable challenge presents itself in the form of Mr. Gupta, the owner of a prominent electronics OEM (Original Equipment Manufacturer). Gupta's initial skepticism towards a relatively small and untested manufacturing firm is a formidable hurdle that Vikram Sharma is determined to overcome.

As Vikram and Rajan navigate the intricacies of their business, Vikram is keenly aware of the potential game-changer that securing Gupta's trust could be for DynaGrow. Gupta, a seasoned player in the electronics industry, has consistently eluded Rajan during his Delhi days in the business world. Convincing him to consider DynaGrow as a viable OEM partner will be no easy feat.

Their first encounter is at a local business event. Vikram extends a friendly greeting to Mr. Gupta, who responds with a skeptical tone, questioning what a relatively unknown company like DynaGrow could offer that established manufacturers couldn't. Vikram, undeterred, explains their commitment to quality and expresses his eagerness to understand Gupta's OEM needs better.

In this critical endeavor, Vikram takes the lead, dedicating countless hours to unravel Gupta's business intricacies, aspirations, and concerns. He doesn't approach Gupta as a mere seller but as a partner in their mutual pursuit of success. Vikram's humility in acknowledging Gupta's expertise and his eagerness to learn from him leaves a lasting impression on Gupta.

But building trust is no easy task. Gupta's reservations stem from past experiences with smaller OEMs that have often fallen short in terms of capacity and reliability. He cautiously shares these concerns with Vikram during a follow-up phone call. Vikram, always empathetic, assures Gupta that DynaGrow is determined to change that perception and suggests collaborating on a small project to showcase their commitment to quality.

Vikram's dedication to winning Gupta's confidence is evident when he organizes a factory tour for Gupta to witness their advanced facilities. Gupta, impressed by the infrastructure, can't help but raise concerns about the scale of his OEM orders. Vikram, brimming with confidence, assures him that DynaGrow is well-equipped to handle his orders, with the latest technology and a skilled workforce at their disposal.

Their interactions aren't limited to formal meetings. Over dinner at a business conference, Gupta, now noticeably more relaxed, admits, "You know, Vikram, you've been persistent. I've decided to give DynaGrow a chance with a small OEM order." Vikram, visibly excited, thanks Gupta for his trust and pledges that they will embark on this OEM journey together.

But Vikram's strategy extends beyond business meetings and negotiations. He understands the value of building a genuine rapport with Gupta. They meet not only in boardrooms but across various cities and even socially, where business discussions often take a back seat to personal connections. These interactions allow Gupta to see Vikram's character and values beyond the confines of their professional relationship.

Over time, Gupta begins to admire Vikram not only for his professional acumen but also for his integrity and dedication. Gupta, a shrewd businessman himself, recognizes in Vikram a kindred spirit who values honesty and commitment. Their conversations evolve from purely business matters to discussions about life, philosophy, and the intricacies of running successful enterprises.

As the years pass, Vikram and Gupta's relationship deepens. Vikram, ever the eager learner, finds in Gupta a mentor who generously shares his business acumen and insights. Gupta's guidance proves invaluable, helping Vikram hone his leadership skills and strategic thinking. Their mentorship transcends the boundaries of business, as Gupta imparts lessons that extend far beyond the confines of their industry.

One evening, during a dinner gathering, Gupta looks at Vikram with a warm smile and says, "You know, Vikram, I've seen your commitment not just to business but to personal growth. You've earned my trust, not just as a business partner but more as a friend. I believe in your potential to lead not just in our industry but beyond it."

Vikram, filled with gratitude, thanks Gupta for his trust and guidance. Gupta's belief in Vikram's abilities is a turning point in their relationship. It is a testament to the power of trust, perseverance, and genuine connections in the world of business.

Their journey from skepticism to trust has been marked by persistence, determination, and the unwavering commitment to building a genuine relationship. Gupta's decision to place that initial OEM order is not merely a business transaction; it is a symbol of the connection they have forged over the years. It is a partnership that goes beyond contracts and invoices, driven by mutual respect and the shared pursuit of excellence.

As Gupta's initial order finds its way onto their production line, a palpable sense of excitement fills the air at DynaGrow Ventures. Rajan, in particular, feels a surge of pride for finally securing the client who had eluded him during his Delhi days in the business world. It is a personal victory for him, a testament to his technical prowess and his unwavering belief in the capabilities of DynaGrow.

Rajan can't help but admire Vikram's persistence and the genuine rapport he has built with Gupta over time. He realizes that it is Vikram's humility, dedication, and relentless pursuit of excellence that has paved the way for this significant milestone. Rajan, often reserved in his emotions, can't help but express his admiration for Vikram's tenacity.

"Vikram," he says one evening during a late-night strategy session, "I've always believed in the quality of our work, but your ability to build these relationships is remarkable. Gupta's trust in us is a testament to your dedication. Let's make sure we not only meet but exceed his expectations."

Vikram, with a warm smile, acknowledges Rajan's words. He knows that this partnership is not just about fulfilling Gupta's order but about setting a precedent for the numerous clients they hope to acquire in the future. It is about delivering excellence consistently, regardless of the challenges that lay ahead.

And challenges do come their way. Late-night strategy sessions become a norm as Vikram and Rajan chart the course for DynaGrow's growth. Production hiccups are addressed with precision, and customer relationships are nurtured with utmost care. The capricious nature of the market tests their resilience, but it also sharpens their adaptability.

Soon, word of DynaGrow's commitment to quality and their unwavering dedication to customer satisfaction spreads like wildfire. Gupta, once a skeptic, becomes a vocal advocate for the company. His confidence in DynaGrow not only solidifies but also opens doors to new opportunities. Other clients, witnessing the success of Gupta's projects, seek out DynaGrow for their manufacturing needs.

Vikram and Rajan's partnership evolves into a dynamic force that not only meets the expectations of clients but consistently exceeds them. Their ability to balance Vikram's visionary outlook with Rajan's technical excellence becomes a hallmark of DynaGrow's success. It isn't just about one client; it is about the reputation they are building in the industry.

Their journey from skepticism to trust has indeed been transformative, not just for Gupta but for the entire trajectory of DynaGrow Ventures. It is a journey that showcases the power of perseverance, humility, and the unwavering pursuit of excellence in the world of business.

Nonetheless, their journey is far from a smooth sail, punctuated by late-night strategy sessions, production hiccups, and the capricious nature of the market. Vikram and Rajan's partnership faces a litany of paradoxes, including the delicate equilibrium between strength and vulnerability and the alignment of their vision with humility.

With the passage of time at DynaGrow Ventures, Vikram and Rajan find themselves at a crossroads, wrestling with the contrasting paradigms that define their approaches. It isn't merely a clash of personalities; it is a clash of visions for the future of their venture.

Vikram, the eternal optimist and extrovert, can't help but spot opportunities at every turn. His knack for identifying market trends and grasping the unspoken desires of their clients transforms his interactions into symphonies of ideas, exchanges brimming with insights and aspirations. He is the dreamer, the visionary who aims for the stars.

In stark contrast, Rajan is the quiet genius who takes solace in numbers and precision. He forms the bedrock of the technical side of their business, ensuring that each product they deliver is an engineering masterpiece. His meticulous nature means that no stone remains unturned in perfecting their existing processes. Change, especially untested change, stirs his unease.

Their conflicting perspectives reach a crescendo when the prospect of expanding their product line looms. Vikram views it as a chance to diversify, to tap into new markets, and to cater to a broader clientele. He brims with excitement about the potential for growth and innovation that this expansion could bring.

Rajan, however, approaches the idea with caution. He harbors reservations about stretching their resources too thin and compromising the quality that has become synonymous with their brand. For him, the age-old adage, "If it ain't broke, don't fix it," holds great weight. He frets that delving into unfamiliar terrain might jeopardize the hard-earned reputation they have established.

The debates that ensue between Vikram and Rajan are not mere discussions; they are passionate clashes of ideologies. Often, they sit in their modest office, surrounded by sketches of new product ideas and spreadsheets detailing production processes. Their debates extend into the late hours of the night, the room resonating with the clinking of coffee mugs and the rustling of papers.

One fateful evening, amidst the remnants of yet another fervent discussion, a revelation strikes them. The very differences that have ignited these debates are the pillars upon which their partnership stands strong. Vikram's visionary outlook perfectly complements Rajan's meticulous planning. Rajan's steadfast commitment to quality provides the grounding for Vikram's boundless enthusiasm.

In a moment of clarity, Vikram utters, "Rajan, it's as though we're two sides of the same coin. Your unwavering focus on quality ensures that our products are top-notch, and my vision propels us to explore new horizons. We need both these facets to succeed."

Rajan nods, fully grasping the profundity of Vikram's words. Their differences are not hurdles to overcome but strengths that fortify DynaGrow's foundation. They are pieces of a puzzle that seamlessly fit together, each contributing to the grander picture.

From that pivotal moment onward, Vikram and Rajan adopt a fresh approach to decision-making. They challenge one another, certainly, but they also listen with open minds. Vikram presents his visionary ideas, and Rajan meticulously scrutinizes them. Rajan voices his concerns, and Vikram responds with pragmatic solutions. It is a delicate dance of collaboration, a harmonious blend of innovation and precision.

Their partnership evolves into a symphony of teamwork. When they choose to diversify their product line, they do so with a resolute commitment to upholding their exacting quality standards. In the face of production setbacks, they don't merely tackle technical issues but also maintain transparent communication with their clients, reaffirming their unwavering dedication to building and nurturing customer relationships.

Ultimately, it is the fusion of Vikram's client-centric approach and Rajan's technical brilliance that propels DynaGrow Ventures onto a trajectory of consistent success within the evolving Indian market of the 1980s and '90s. They emerge as a dynamic duo, their partnership a shining testament to the potent synergy of collaboration and the wisdom of embracing paradoxes in leadership.

Collaborate to Create - A SOAR Perspective

As Vikram's entrepreneurial journey unfolds, a paradox emerges that will become a cornerstone of his leadership philosophy: the delicate interplay between strength and vulnerability. It is a paradox that will not only shape his path but also offer valuable insights into the world of leadership and management.

Vikram is undeniably a force to be reckoned with. His unique strength lies in his innate ability to connect with people. He possesses the uncanny skill of deciphering their needs, dreams, and aspirations. His determination and unwavering commitment to his goals are evident from the very beginning. However, it is his willingness to embrace vulnerability that sets him apart as a leader.

In the world of business, strength is often associated with unwavering confidence and an unyielding resolve. It's the ability to make decisions swiftly and stand firm in the face of challenges. Vikram has these qualities, but he understands that true strength goes beyond surface-level attributes.

Vikram's vulnerability is his secret weapon. He isn't afraid to admit when he lacks answers or when he encounters obstacles he can't surmount alone. Instead of masking his vulnerability, he seeks guidance from his partner, Rajan, and other industry experts. This openness to learning and growth becomes a source of strength in itself.

Vikram Sharma's approach to leadership teaches us that being real about our limits can actually be a strength, helping us connect better with our teams. He believes in always learning and growing, a mindset that pushes both him and his colleagues to keep improving. Vikram knows that different people bring different strengths to the table and that the synergy between Vikram's interpersonal skills and Rajan's technical prowess makes their team stronger together. By being open about not knowing everything, Vikram encourages his team to come up with fresh, creative ideas. It's his humility and willingness to learn from others, including Mr. Gupta, that makes him a trusted leader. And it's the combination of all these traits that makes Vikram and Rajan's partnership so effective.

As Vikram's journey continues, this paradox of strength and vulnerability will be a guiding light in his leadership philosophy. It serves as a reminder that authentic leaders are not infallible heroes but individuals who harness their unique strengths while remaining open to growth and learning. In the intricate dance of strength and vulnerability, Vikram's journey illuminates the path for leaders navigating their own odysseys, proving that paradoxes can be a source of strength rather than contradiction.

Let's navigate these concepts through the SOAR model, offering simple steps that you can integrate into your daily leadership journey:

S - Self-Reflect:

Take some time each day for self-reflection. Identify one area where you feel vulnerable or uncertain in your leadership role. Write down your thoughts and feelings about it, and then brainstorm ways to embrace and leverage that vulnerability as a strength.

O - Own your Journey:

Own your personal and professional development by setting aside dedicated time for learning. Commit to reading one leadership or management book each month or taking an online course. Reflect on what you've learned and how it can be applied in your leadership role.

A - Act with Persistence:

When faced with a challenging problem or project, persistently encourage open dialogue within your team. Create a safe space where team members can share their ideas, even if they are uncertain about them. Actively listen to their input and work collaboratively to explore innovative solutions.

R - Rise Higher:

To rise higher in your leadership journey, practice humility by seeking feedback from your team and colleagues. Regularly ask for their input on your leadership style and areas for improvement. Embrace their feedback with gratitude and use it to continuously refine your leadership approach.

• 27 •

SOAR
S
Self-Reflect
Embrace your Vulnerabilities
O
Own Your Journey
Commit to learn continuously
A
Act With Persistence
Encourage open dialogue to find answers.
R
Rise Higher
Be humble in taking feedback

By aligning these leadership lessons with the SOAR model and taking these simple actions, readers can enhance their leadership skills, foster personal growth, and navigate their leadership journeys with authenticity and resilience.

CHAPTER 3

The Enigmatic Mentor

In the midst of these challenges, a serendipitous encounter changes the course of Vikram's leadership journey. It happens at an industry conference where professionals from various sectors, including Vikram, are invited to participate and share insights and expertise. Vikram is there not only as an eager participant but also as a distinguished panelist, ready to contribute his perspective on critical issues facing businesses today.

The conference buzzes with the energy of innovation and ambition. In a sea of attendees, Vikram finds himself amidst the elite minds of diverse industries, all converging to explore the frontiers of leadership. The air is filled with the exchange of ideas, the clinking of coffee cups, and the anticipation of groundbreaking discussions.

Vikram, distinguished in a sharp suit, takes his place on the panel, which consists of other industry experts and entrepreneurs. Nirmala, a seasoned business consultant and one of the best in the world, is seated to his right. She is known for her exceptional insights into industry dynamics and her remarkable ability to catalyze positive change within companies.

The discussion revolves around the topic of Special Economic Zones (SEZs) and their impact on growing businesses, but Vikram is keen to address a broader spectrum of issues.

He begins, "SEZs offer significant advantages, no doubt. The subsidies, tax benefits, and streamlined operations can indeed catalyze growth." Pausing for effect, he continues, "However, let's not overlook the elephant in the room – the complexities we face in the modern business landscape."

Vikram elaborates, "Integration is a constant challenge. With businesses expanding across borders and domains, ensuring seamless integration of diverse systems and processes can be akin to solving a puzzle with ever-shifting pieces."

Nirmala, the renowned business consultant, acknowledges the point with a nod. She adds, "Indeed, integration is just one facet of the modern business landscape. Data security is paramount. As businesses collect and store vast amounts of data, safeguarding it from cyber threats and breaches becomes an intricate dance of technology and vigilance."

Vikram presses on, "Talent and skill variability is another aspect that can't be ignored. In today's world, finding and retaining top-tier talent with the right skills is a perpetual challenge. It's like searching for a needle in a haystack."

Scalability is his next focus. "And let's not forget scalability challenges," Vikram continues. "While SEZs can provide a fertile ground for growth, scaling operations while maintaining quality and consistency can be a daunting task."

Nirmala adds her expertise, "Lastly, there's the ever-present debate of centralized versus decentralized control. Striking the right balance between efficiency and autonomy can be a tightrope walk."

Their exchange of ideas continues, diving deep into the intricacies of these modern business challenges. As the panel discussion concludes, Vikram and Nirmala find themselves in animated conversation, their shared passion for leadership and innovation serving as a strong foundation for their connection.

The evening sun casts a warm glow over the conference venue as Vikram and Nirmala continue their discussion over dinner in the conclave. The atmosphere is convivial, with the clinking of cutlery and the soft hum of conversation providing a soothing backdrop to their conversation.

Vikram, now deeply engrossed in the topics they had touched upon during the panel discussion, leans in and says, "Nirmala, I must admit that your insights into these complexities are truly enlightening. It's refreshing to meet someone who not only understands the challenges but also appreciates their impact on business growth."

Nirmala, her eyes reflecting a genuine passion for her work, replies, "Thank you, Vikram. I believe that recognizing these challenges is the first step towards finding innovative solutions. And I've seen firsthand how addressing these complexities can lead to transformative change within organizations."

Vikram can't help but feel a deep sense of respect for Nirmala. Her wisdom, experience, and genuine commitment to making a difference leave a lasting impression on him. He admires not only her expertise but also her willingness to share it and her eagerness to collaborate.

As they continue their dialogue, Vikram broaches the subject of DynaGrow's expansion plans with a sense of trust in Nirmala's guidance. "Nirmala, I have a situation at DynaGrow that I believe aligns with the very challenges we've been discussing today. We've been offered an opportunity to expand to a new location, one that comes with significant tax incentives that could greatly benefit us financially. However, the complexities in integrating our operations, ensuring data security, finding the right talent, and scaling up while maintaining quality are daunting."

He continues, "I've been pondering on how to navigate these challenges effectively, and I couldn't help but think of your expertise. Would you consider providing us with a consultation? Your guidance could be invaluable in helping us make the right decisions and charting a successful expansion strategy."

Nirmala, always open to opportunities where she can make a meaningful impact, regards Vikram with a thoughtful gaze. "Vikram," she replies with a warm smile, "I'm honored that you would consider me for such an important role. Your dedication to addressing these challenges aligns perfectly with my passion for catalyzing positive change. I would be delighted to work with you and DynaGrow Ventures to navigate these complexities and ensure a successful expansion."

In that moment, their mutual respect for each other's expertise and their shared commitment to tackling the complexities of leadership and business growth solidify their partnership. It is the beginning of a collaboration that holds the promise of transformative change and a brighter future for DynaGrow Ventures.

Over the following months, Vikram and Nirmala embark on a journey together, navigating the complexities of setting up DynaGrow's new manufacturing unit. What begins as a consulting project evolves into a life-changing mentorship, one that will leave an indelible mark on both of their leadership journeys.

Nirmala, with her wealth of experience and exceptional insights, coaches Vikram through the intricate process of integrating the new unit with the existing operations. They tackle the challenges of data security by implementing cutting-edge cybersecurity measures, ensuring that DynaGrow's sensitive information remains safeguarded.

The quest for talent and skills leads them to innovative recruiting strategies, leveraging Nirmala's extensive network and Vikram's innate ability to connect with potential candidates on a personal level. Together, they assemble a team of talented individuals who not only possess the required skills but also share DynaGrow's vision and values.

Scaling up the new unit while maintaining quality is a delicate balancing act that Vikram and Nirmala approach with meticulous planning and a commitment to excellence. They establish robust processes, emphasizing efficiency without compromising on product quality. Vikram's dedication to maintaining DynaGrow's reputation for excellence resonates with Nirmala, who admires his unwavering commitment to the highest standards.

As the months pass, Vikram's respect for Nirmala deepens. He observes her coaching style closely, learning not only from her expertise but also from her humility and dedication to their shared mission. Nirmala, in turn, looks at Vikram with a sense of pride and affection. She sees in him a dutiful student and a mentee who not only absorbs knowledge but applies it with a sense of purpose.

As the consulting project nears its completion, the new manufacturing unit stands as a testament to their collaboration—a cutting-edge facility ready to propel DynaGrow to new heights in the industry.

During the project's closing meeting, Nirmala addresses Vikram and the DynaGrow team. "It has been an incredible journey, one marked by dedication and a relentless pursuit of excellence," she begins. "Vikram, your leadership and commitment have been exceptional. I have no doubt that DynaGrow's new unit will not only succeed but also set a new standard in the industry."

She continues, "I've had the privilege of working with many talented individuals in my career, but I see in you, Vikram, the potential to lead DynaGrow to unprecedented heights on a global scale. Your thirst for knowledge, your dedication to your team, and your unwavering commitment to excellence set you apart as a remarkable leader."

Nirmala's words resonate deeply with Vikram. He has not only gained a mentor but also a champion who believes in his potential to lead DynaGrow to greatness.

As the consulting project officially concludes, Nirmala makes a decision that will shape Vikram's leadership journey even further. She approaches him with a proposition, "Vikram, our consulting contract may have ended, but I believe there's more for us to explore together. I would like to continue coaching you personally, to help you prepare for the new heights you're about to scale as a leader."

Vikram, deeply moved by Nirmala's offer, accepts without hesitation. Their coaching continues, transcending the boundaries of business. It becomes a partnership built on mutual respect, trust, and a shared vision of leadership excellence.

In the months and years that follow, Vikram continues to steer DynaGrow with Nirmala's coaching, achieving remarkable growth and innovation. Nirmala's belief in him and her unwavering support become pillars of his leadership journey, propelling him toward a future where DynaGrow will indeed lead the industry globally, and where he will stand as a testament to the transformative power of coaching and leadership excellence.

Under Nirmala's expert coaching, Vikram's leadership journey continues to evolve, and their coaching sessions become a cherished ritual in his pursuit of excellence.

One of the most important lessons Nirmala imparts to Vikram is the significance of vulnerability in leadership. She doesn't just talk about it; she embodies it in every interaction they share. She opens up about her own struggles, setbacks, and moments of doubt, dispelling the misconception that leaders have to be infallible. Through her candid stories, Vikram realizes that leadership isn't about being invulnerable; it's about acknowledging one's vulnerabilities and recognizing the need for support.

Their coaching sessions often unfold in a cozy corner of a local café, where the aroma of freshly brewed coffee seems to infuse their conversations with warmth and wisdom. Nirmala creates a safe space for Vikram to discuss his insecurities and doubts, encouraging self-reflection as a crucial aspect of leadership growth.

Vikram soon discovers that vulnerability is a powerful tool for building trust within his team. By openly sharing his own challenges and uncertainties, he creates an environment where others feel empowered to do the same. This newfound openness leads to deeper connections among team members and fosters a culture of mutual support within DynaGrow Ventures.

As Vikram delves deeper into his coaching with Nirmala, he undergoes a marked shift in his perception of mistakes. Nirmala stresses the importance of learning from errors and adapting swiftly. It is a perspective that Vikram wholeheartedly embraces and carries into his leadership style. He encourages his team to view setbacks not as failures but as valuable lessons and stepping stones on the path to success.

The ripple effect of Vikram's transformation through vulnerability is palpable within DynaGrow Ventures. Inspired by their leader's authenticity, team members begin to embrace their own vulnerabilities. They share ideas freely, without fear of judgment, and collaborate more effectively. Challenges are no longer perceived as obstacles but as opportunities to learn and grow.

As Vikram continues to evolve as a leader, he knows that embracing vulnerability will remain a cornerstone of his leadership philosophy. It is a philosophy that not only enriches his own growth but also continues to shape the culture and effectiveness of DynaGrow Ventures. Under Nirmala's tutelage, Vikram is not only becoming a better leader but also a beacon of inspiration for those around him, and the journey is far from over.

The Balancing Act: A SOAR Perspective

In the ever-evolving landscape of leadership, one paradox reigns supreme: the interplay between strength and vulnerability. It's a paradox that we often find reflected in the most remarkable leaders, a delicate dance between seemingly opposing qualities. Vikram's journey serves as a compelling narrative to illustrate the transformative potential of this paradox.

At the outset of his leadership journey, Vikram embodies the quintessential image of strength. As a distinguished panelist at a prestigious conference, he radiates confidence and ambition. He is the embodiment of a leader who has conquered numerous challenges and achieved success. Strength is his armor, shielding him from doubt and vulnerability.

However, it is precisely at this point, amidst the applause and accolades, that a subtle yet distinct transformation begins. It is a transformation catalyzed by an encounter with Nirmala, a seasoned management consultant. Nirmala's wisdom and experience hint at a deeper understanding of leadership—one that transcends the façade of unyielding strength.

Through his interactions with Nirmala, Vikram gradually starts to appreciate the value of authenticity. He discovers that vulnerability isn't a sign of weakness but a source of immense power. It is the willingness to admit uncertainties, ask for help when needed, and reveal one's authentic self to others. It is a trait that creates connections, builds trust, and fosters a culture of openness within teams.

The paradox is unfolding before Vikram's eyes. He sees that true strength lies in the courage to be vulnerable. It is the strength to say, "I don't have all the answers," the strength to acknowledge mistakes, and the strength to seek support and feedback from others. This newfound understanding revolutionizes his leadership philosophy.

As Vikram's journey continues, he finds himself embracing vulnerability more and more. He understands that leadership is not about projecting an invincible image but about connecting with others on a human level. Vulnerability becomes his bridge to authenticity—a quality that resonates deeply with his team members.

His transformation has a ripple effect. Team members, inspired by Vikram's authenticity, begin to embrace their vulnerabilities as well. They share their ideas, concerns, and challenges without fear of judgment. This culture of openness leads to improved problem-solving, innovation, and a stronger sense of unity within DynaGrow Ventures.

Vikram's journey underscores a vital management lesson: the paradox of strength and vulnerability is not a choice between one or the other but a harmonious fusion of both. The strongest leaders are those who can confidently wield their strength while remaining open to vulnerability. They acknowledge their limitations, learn from their mistakes, and foster a culture of trust and collaboration.

Let's navigate these concepts through the SOAR model, offering simple steps that you can integrate into your daily leadership journey:

S - Self-Reflect:

Set aside time each week for self-reflection. Journal about your leadership experiences, challenges, and moments of vulnerability. Consider how these moments have influenced your leadership style.

O - Own your Journey:

Create a personal leadership development plan. Identify specific areas where you can improve and set achievable goals. Regularly revisit and adjust your plan as you progress.

A - Act with Persistence:

Commit to open and honest communication with your team. Encourage them to share their thoughts and concerns. Even when faced with challenges, persist in creating an environment where vulnerability is valued.

R - Rise Higher:

Seek mentorship or coaching from a seasoned leader who can guide you in balancing strength and vulnerability. Actively apply the insights gained to rise higher as a leader while staying grounded in authenticity.

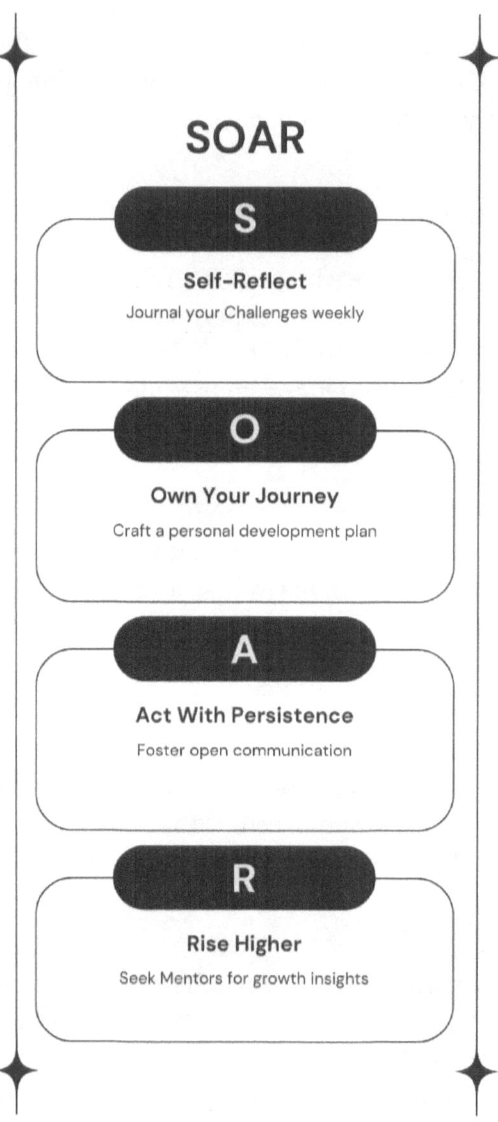

SOAR
S
Self-Reflect
Journal your Challenges weekly
O
Own Your Journey
Craft a personal development plan
A
Act With Persistence
Foster open communication
R
Rise Higher
Seek Mentors for growth insights

By integrating these actions into your leadership journey, you can effectively navigate the paradox of strength and vulnerability, fostering a more authentic and impactful leadership style.

In a world where leadership is constantly evolving, leaders who embrace this paradox are better equipped to navigate complexity, build resilient teams, and drive lasting success. Vikram's journey serves as a testament to the power of paradox in leadership—a power that can transform not only individuals but entire organizations, propelling them toward a brighter and more innovative future.

Embracing Paradoxes

CHAPTER 4

The Birth of Innovation

Rajan's journey mirrors Vikram's in its quest for growth and transformation. Yet, while Vikram thrived in the spotlight of leadership, Rajan is a more introspective soul. He is the quiet genius, deeply immersed in the world of technology and innovation.

With an unwavering focus, Rajan delves into the intricate details of his field. He dedicates himself to understanding the core knowledge and the nuances of technology. While Vikram steers the ship, Rajan is the engine, churning out one innovation after another.

Rajan's approach to managing people is unique. He impresses them not with charisma or grand gestures but with his sheer authority on the subject matter. He is a mentor in the truest sense, guiding his team through complex challenges while nurturing their learning and growth.

Within DynaGrow, Rajan earns a reputation as the subject matter expert, a title not given lightly. His insights and problem-solving abilities are revered by his colleagues. It isn't just his technical acumen that sets him apart; it's his ability to break down complex concepts into understandable pieces that make him an invaluable asset.

Teams within DynaGrow often seek Rajan for technical issues and to further their learning. He patiently shares his knowledge, helping them navigate the intricacies of technology and innovation. His office becomes a sanctuary of ideas and exploration.

As Rajan's reputation grows, so do his responsibilities. His expertise extends beyond the walls of DynaGrow, reaching the academic world. He is invited to serve as an advisor to multiple university research projects, where his insights illuminate new paths of discovery.

However, Rajan's newfound role as an advisor also comes with its own demands. His calendar fills with meetings, presentations, and consultations. The demands of being a subject matter expert begin to occupy a significant portion of his time.

Amidst this whirlwind of opportunities and responsibilities, Vikram, always attuned to the needs of the company, recognizes the need for balance. With Rajan deeply engrossed in his advisory roles, Vikram takes on additional responsibilities within the company's operations.

Vikram's ability to adapt and lead is evident as he seamlessly manages the day-to-day affairs of DynaGrow. His leadership style, shaped by the mentorship of Nirmala, evolves to encompass not only strategic vision but also effective operations management.

The teams at DynaGrow find their mentors within the organization. They go to Rajan for technical issues and to deepen their understanding of technology and innovation. Rajan patiently shares his knowledge, helping them solve intricate problems and fostering a culture of continuous learning.

In contrast, when dilemmas, conflicts, or trust-based issues arise, the teams turn to Vikram. His open-door policy and empathetic leadership style make him a trusted confidant. He approaches each challenge as an opportunity for growth, nurturing an environment where transparency and trust thrive.

The synergy between Vikram and Rajan remains a cornerstone of DynaGrow's success. While Rajan's technical brilliance propels the company to new heights, Vikram's leadership ensures the ship sails smoothly. Together, they form an unbreakable partnership that defines the essence of DynaGrow.

In the early days, Rajan solves technical issues for clients out of sheer interest. He relishes the thrill of deciphering complex problems and finding ingenious solutions. These endeavors, fueled by passion, often result in solutions that exceed client expectations.

Rajan, with his innate curiosity and appetite for learning, keenly observes Vikram's adaptability and how Nirmala's guidance played a pivotal role in shaping not only Vikram but also the trajectory of DynaGrow. Being a natural learner, Rajan expresses his desire to join one of their coaching sessions to further his own growth.

With a welcoming nod from Vikram and a warm smile from Nirmala, Rajan becomes a periodic participant in their coaching meetings. He immerses himself in their discussions, absorbing leadership insights and strategies. Through these interactions, Rajan gains a deeper appreciation for the intricacies of leadership, strategy, and organizational dynamics.

As Rajan continues to join their coaching sessions, the bond between the three of them grows stronger. They share their journeys, challenges, and triumphs, learning from one another's experiences. Rajan's perspective as a subject matter expert adds a unique dimension to their conversations, enriching the discussions with technical insights.

It is during one of these coaching sessions that the idea of creating a specialized business unit within DynaGrow begins to take shape. Nirmala, always attuned to the dynamics of the organization, recognizes the untapped potential in Rajan's remarkable technical prowess.

During a strategy session with Vikram and Rajan, Nirmala presents her idea. "Rajan," she begins, "your ability to tackle technical challenges is truly remarkable. I've seen how your innovations have not only solved problems but also enhanced our products and services. I believe it's time to give your passion a dedicated space within DynaGrow."

Vikram, ever the visionary, sees the potential immediately. "Nirmala, you're absolutely right," he concurs. "Rajan's technical genius deserves a platform of its own. Let's create a specialized unit within DynaGrow, a place where industry leaders can come to seek answers to their most pressing technical challenges."

The idea resonates deeply with Rajan, who had not only witnessed Vikram's adaptability but had also experienced the transformative power of Nirmala's coaching. With enthusiasm in his voice, Rajan adds, "I believe this could be an opportunity not only to further our technical capabilities but also to inspire innovation and problem-solving across industries."

And so, the seeds of innovation are sown, and the vision for DynaGrow's specialized business unit begins to take root. It is a testament to the power of collaboration, learning, and recognizing untapped potential within an organization.

With that, the wheels are set in motion. Together, Vikram and Rajan embark on a journey to transform Rajan's passion into a thriving business unit. They meticulously plan every detail, from assembling a team of technical experts to defining the unit's mission and goals.

As the technical services unit takes shape, industry stalwarts begin to take notice. They see in DynaGrow's new venture a source of innovative solutions and technical excellence. Rajan's reputation as a problem solver grows, and soon, the unit becomes a go-to destination for companies seeking cutting-edge solutions to their technical dilemmas.

Amidst the excitement of this new venture, Vikram and Rajan's dynamic partnership comes to the forefront once again. Their interactions during this phase are a testament to their enduring synergy and their ability to complement each other's strengths.

One sunny afternoon, as they sit in Vikram's office, overlooking the bustling activity within DynaGrow, Vikram raises a question that has been on his mind. "Rajan, our technical services unit is flourishing, but I've been thinking about our long-term strategy. How can we ensure sustained growth and innovation in this rapidly evolving landscape?"

Rajan, ever the analytical thinker, leans forward and responds, "Vikram, you're right; we need to plan for the future. To ensure sustained growth, we should consider investing in research and development. This will allow us to stay at the forefront of technology and continue to offer cutting-edge solutions to our clients."

Vikram nods in agreement, appreciating Rajan's insight. "R&D sounds like a solid strategy," he replies. "But we should also think about expanding our market reach. Perhaps we can explore international partnerships and collaborations to tap into new opportunities."

As they explore these ideas further, their perspectives occasionally diverge, but their commitment to finding common ground remains unwavering. They engage in healthy debates, considering the pros and cons of each strategy. It is in these moments of constructive conflict that their partnership grows even stronger.

One evening, as they review their progress, Rajan brings up a potential challenge. "Vikram, I've noticed that some team members in our technical unit are feeling overwhelmed by the increasing workload. We need to address this issue to maintain the quality of our work."

Vikram nods, acknowledging the concern. "You're right, Rajan. We must ensure that our team is not overburdened. Let's work on restructuring our teams and possibly hiring additional talent to support our growth."

Their ability to openly discuss challenges and find solutions together is a hallmark of their partnership. It is this synergy that has been the driving force behind DynaGrow's success from its inception.

Over time, they implement a multi-pronged strategy that includes investments in research and development, international collaborations, and a focus on team well-being. These decisions bear fruit as the technical services unit continues to thrive, consistently delivering innovative solutions and exceeding client expectations.

The magic of the initial days of their entrepreneurial journey has not only remained intact but has grown stronger with the years of partnering in DynaGrow. Vikram and Rajan's synergy continues to be a source of inspiration, not just for their team but for the entire organization. It is a testament to the power of collaboration, the value of diverse perspectives, and the enduring strength of their partnership.

Their journey is marked by the birth of innovation within DynaGrow. Rajan's path, like Vikram's, is a testament to the power of passion and purpose. Under the guidance of Nirmala's astute vision, DynaGrow expands its horizons, becoming a hub of technical excellence and a trusted partner to industries far and wide.

As the story of DynaGrow continues to unfold, Vikram, Rajan, and their dedicated team look toward the future with unwavering determination. The pursuit of excellence is their compass, and together, they are poised to lead not only their industry but also the world into a brighter and more innovative tomorrow.

The Drive with a Heart - The SOAR Perspective

In the ever-evolving landscape of leadership, where challenges and opportunities intertwine, the paradox of "Ambition and Empathy" emerges as a guiding light. This paradox teaches us invaluable lessons about effective leadership.

Ambition Drives Success. It is the fuel that propels leaders forward, igniting their desire to achieve greatness. Vikram's story reflects this vital element of leadership. He envisions growth, innovation, and a thriving future for DynaGrow. His ambition drives him to explore new horizons, seize opportunities, and expand the company's reach.

In the pursuit of excellence, ambition keeps leaders focused, determined, and resilient in the face of adversity. Vikram's leadership style mirrors this ambition, as he leads DynaGrow into uncharted territories, where innovation becomes a way of life.

Empathy sits at the heart of leadership even as ambition drives success. Yet, the paradox deepens when ambition works in combination with empathy—a harmonizing symphony reflecting the human aspect. Empathy is the ability to understand and connect with others on a personal level. Vikram exemplifies this by creating an environment where individuals feel heard, valued, and supported.

Vikram's open-door policy and his willingness to listen to his team's dilemmas, conflicts, and trust-based issues demonstrate the significance of empathy in leadership. He recognizes that while ambition fuels progress, empathy fuels relationships. It nurtures a culture of mutual support, fostering an atmosphere where everyone's voice matters.

The lesson from Vikram's journey is clear: effective leadership requires a delicate balance between ambition and empathy. Ambition without empathy risks becoming ruthless pursuit, leaving individuals behind. Empathy without ambition may lead to stagnation, as leaders hesitate to embrace change and growth.

Balancing these qualities means combining the drive to succeed with a deep understanding of the human experience. It means setting audacious goals while nurturing an environment of trust and collaboration. Leaders who strike this balance inspire their teams to reach new heights, fostering a culture of innovation, resilience, and inclusivity.

As you navigate your own leadership journey, remember Vikram's example. Embrace your ambition, set your sights on ambitious goals, and strive for excellence. But never forget the human element—cultivate empathy, connect with your team on a personal level, and create a workplace where both ambition and empathy coexist.

Let's navigate these concepts through the SOAR model, offering simple steps that you can integrate into your daily leadership journey:

S - Self-Reflect: Take time each week to reflect on your leadership journey. Ask yourself how your ambition has driven your actions and how empathy has influenced your relationships with your team. Journal your insights and areas for growth.

O - Own your Journey: Take ownership of balancing ambition and empathy in your leadership style. Recognize that it's a continuous journey. Engage in regular self-assessment and seek feedback from your team to ensure you're effectively balancing these qualities.

A - Act with Persistence: Consistently act on your ambition by setting challenging goals for your team and organization. Simultaneously, act with persistence in cultivating empathy by actively listening to your team's concerns and supporting their growth.

R - Rise Higher: Aim to rise higher by not only achieving your ambitious goals but also by elevating your team's well-being and cohesion through empathy-driven leadership. Encourage your team to rise higher alongside you by fostering an environment where ambition and empathy thrive in harmony.

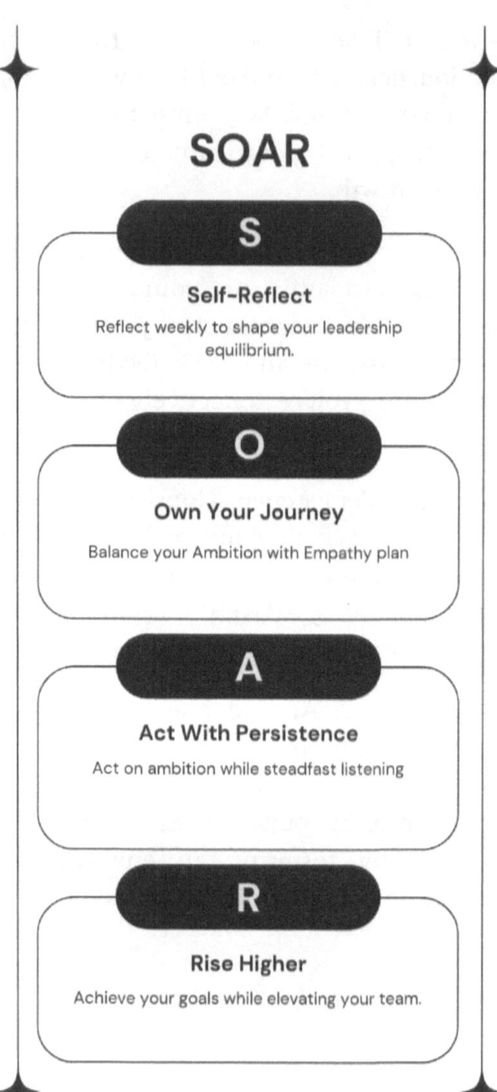
SOAR
S
Self-Reflect
Reflect weekly to shape your leadership equilibrium.
O
Own Your Journey
Balance your Ambition with Empathy plan
A
Act With Persistence
Act on ambition while steadfast listening
R
Rise Higher
Achieve your goals while elevating your team.

By integrating these actions into your leadership journey, you'll be well on your way to balancing ambition and empathy effectively, creating a leadership style that inspires both individual and organizational growth.

In the end, it's the fusion of ambition and empathy that propels leaders, like Vikram, to not only lead their industries but also to shape a brighter and more innovative future. This paradox is the compass that guides leaders toward transformative success, where ambition and empathy walk hand in hand, lighting the path forward.

CHAPTER 5

The Disaster Strikes

The anticipation at DynaGrow was palpable as the company's 30th-anniversary milestone approached. It was a momentous occasion that called for a celebration of three decades of innovation, growth, and transformation. The entire organization buzzed with excitement, and a special committee had been formed to plan a month-long festivity that would befit the occasion.

As the sun dipped below the horizon, casting a warm golden glow over DynaGrow's headquarters, Vikram and Rajan found themselves in the midst of an extraordinary meeting. Gathered around a polished teak table were members of the celebration committee, representing teams from both business units of the company.

The committee consisted of passionate individuals who had a shared commitment to making the 30th-anniversary celebration unforgettable. They hailed from diverse departments, from marketing and operations to research and development. Each member brought their unique perspective and expertise to the table, making it a formidable team.

The room was adorned with colorful banners and posters showcasing DynaGrow's journey over the past 30 years. Photographs captured moments of triumph, innovation, and camaraderie, reminding everyone of the company's remarkable history.

Vikram, with his signature blend of humility and enthusiasm, addressed the committee. "Ladies and gentlemen," he began, his voice resonating with gratitude, "I am truly humbled by the dedication and passion that each of you brings to this celebration committee. Our 30th anniversary is not just a milestone; it's a testament to the collective effort and unwavering commitment of every DynaGrow family member."

Rajan, ever the technical visionary, chimed in, "Indeed, this is a moment for us to reflect on how far we've come and the incredible innovations that have shaped our journey. Let's not only celebrate our past achievements but also set our sights on an even more innovative future."

The committee members nodded in agreement, their faces reflecting a shared determination to make the celebration extraordinary.

One member, Anika, the head of marketing, spoke up, "Vikram, Rajan, we have some exciting ideas for the celebration. We're planning a series of events throughout the month, including knowledge-sharing sessions, innovation showcases, and community engagement activities. It's a chance for us to not only celebrate internally but also connect with our industry peers and the community."

Another committee member, Ravi, who led the research and development team, added, "In addition to the events, we're considering a special edition publication that captures DynaGrow's journey, complete with insights from thought leaders in our industry. It would be a valuable resource for our peers and a testament to our commitment to knowledge-sharing."

Vikram's eyes sparkled with enthusiasm as he listened to the ideas pouring in. "These suggestions are fantastic," he remarked. "Let's ensure that we create an experience that reflects our values, our commitment to innovation, and our gratitude to our employees and partners."

The committee's brainstorming session continued late into the evening, fueled by creativity and a shared sense of purpose. It was clear that the 30th-anniversary celebration would be a month-long extravaganza that not only celebrated the past but also laid the foundation for a future filled with innovation and growth.

As the meeting concluded, Vikram and Rajan exchanged glances, filled with pride and gratitude for the passionate team they had assembled. The stage was set for an unforgettable celebration of DynaGrow's 30 years of excellence.

Vikram and Rajan find themselves at a posh restaurant after the committee meeting, their surroundings bathed in the soft glow of ambient lighting.

Vikram leans back in his chair, a playful glint in his eye. "Rajan, you remember the days when we were just a couple of dreamers in that colony park, right?"

Rajan chuckles, a hint of nostalgia in his voice. "Ah, those were the days, Vikram. We were full of ideas and had no clue what we were getting into."

Vikram grins. "Yeah, we were like, 'Let's conquer the world!' without even a map."

Rajan's gaze drifts to the flickering candle on the table. "You know, it's not just our business that's grown. Our families have, too. Healthy, happy homes, thanks to this rollercoaster ride."

Vikram nods, his thoughts on his own family. "You bet. They've been the cheerleaders in our crazy game."

Rajan looks back at Vikram, a mischievous glimmer in his eye. "And speaking of games, who would've thought our dream would become this massive league?"

Vikram laughs. "True, Rajan. We've got our own championship team now."

The two friends banter and reminisce, their laughter filling the air. The years have brought them success, but their camaraderie remains unchanged.

As they prepare to leave, Vikram slaps Rajan on the back with a grin. "Don't expect me bright and early tomorrow. I've earned myself a sleep-in."

"You've got it. Enjoy the rest, coach."

With that, they head their separate ways, their bond stronger than ever, ready to take on whatever the future holds.

In the dimly lit room of their home, Vikram is lost in the deep embrace of sleep. The events of the celebration committee meeting and the jovial dinner with Rajan seem like distant memories. His rhythmic breathing is the only sound that fills the room.

But the tranquility of the morning breaks abruptly by a nudge. Priya, his wife, stands beside the bed, her face drained of color. She hesitates for a moment, knowing what lies ahead will be shattering. With a deep breath, she gently nudges Vikram awake, her phone trembling in her hand.

Vikram's eyes flutter open, and as they meet Priya's pale, worried face, a sense of dread washes over him. Without uttering a single word, Priya hands him the phone. It takes only a minute, but the conversation on the other end leaves Vikram white as a sheet.

In that moment, there are no words shared between husband and wife. They both understand the gravity of the situation. Their minds go into overdrive, racing through what needs to be done.

Without a word, they dress and make their way out of the house, their steps heavy with the weight of the impending crisis. It's a situation neither of them had ever imagined facing, one that will test their resilience and leadership in ways they couldn't foresee.

As they drive towards the heart of the disaster, the streets are still cloaked in the quiet of the early morning. Vikram's mind goes into autopilot. His emotions shut down temporarily, replaced by a steely resolve to deal with the multiple aspects of the impending crisis.

This time, when the news about DynaGrow makes headlines, it's a stark departure from the celebratory tone of the 30th-anniversary planning. The company's resilience and spirit will be put to the test in ways they could never have anticipated, as they face a disaster that will challenge their leadership and the very core of their organization.

Vikram's heart races as he arrives at the scene, the towering plumes of smoke blotting out the sun. The cacophony of sirens and the deafening roar of the fire engines add to the chaos. Donning a fire-resistant suit and helmet, he joins the ranks of seasoned firefighters, their faces smudged with soot and determination etched into their expressions.

The heat is oppressive, like a relentless furnace, and sweat mixed with soot drips down Vikram's face. Each step towards the inferno feels like a step closer to an unimaginable abyss. The flames, fueled by chemicals and machinery, leap and dance with an almost malevolent intent.

Vikram's gloved hands grip a hose with white-knuckled intensity as he and his comrades direct torrents of water and foam toward the relentless fire. The intensity of the battle is surreal, as if they are combating an elemental force. Embers, like fiery butterflies, swirl in the air, casting an eerie, otherworldly glow. It's a moment where time seems to stretch, each second an eternity in the struggle to control the blaze.

Amidst the chaos, the focus shifts to rescue and recovery. The frantic cries for help pierce through the roar of the fire. Firefighters and emergency personnel rush into the building, their faces obscured by breathing masks, their actions swift and calculated.

Vikram witnesses acts of heroism that will remain etched in his memory forever. A firefighter emerges from the smoke, cradling a terrified employee in their arms. A group of colleagues forms a human chain to guide others to safety through the blinding haze. It's a symphony of bravery and selflessness, a testament to the human spirit's resilience in the face of calamity.

As the injured are evacuated, Vikram can't escape the haunting images of their faces—faces etched with pain, fear, and shock. He visits the hospitals where they are receiving medical care, offering words of solace to the wounded and their families. The stark reality of the disaster hits him like a sledgehammer.

Rajan, on the other hand, has been rendered almost speechless by the magnitude of the disaster. He wanders through the wreckage in a daze, his mind unable to process the enormity of the situation. As the night wears on, the shock and trauma take their toll, and he collapses, unresponsive to the chaos around him. Emergency responders quickly rush him to the hospital for medical attention.

With the fire finally under control and the injured receiving medical care, Vikram finds himself standing before a sea of cameras and microphones. His face is etched with weariness, but his voice remains steady as he addresses the reporters who clamor for information. He provides updates on the situation, his words measured and empathetic.

Behind the composed exterior, Vikram carries the weight of responsibility for the disaster. Questions and accusations swirl around him, and he bears them with grace, recognizing that accountability is an essential step toward healing and recovery. It's a moment where leadership means bearing the weight of the world on one's shoulders.

As the night wears on, Vikram retreats from the chaos. He finds a quiet corner amidst the charred debris and sits down, his body and mind weary from the relentless battle. Soot-streaked tears mix with the dirt on his face as he allows himself a moment of vulnerability.

The enormity of the loss and the trauma of the day wash over him like a tidal wave. He thinks of the employees who have perished, their faces and voices haunting his thoughts. The weight of leadership and the responsibility for their safety bear down on him, and he questions whether he could have done more.

As the first light of dawn breaks through the smoke, casting a somber, ashen glow over the scene, Vikram knows that the road to recovery will be long and arduous. The disaster has left an indelible mark on DynaGrow and its employees. But amidst the ashes and ruins, he sees a glimmer of hope.

The resilience of the human spirit, the unwavering bravery of first responders, and the unity of the DynaGrow family are reminders that even in the darkest hours, there is a strength that cannot be extinguished. It's a testament to the indomitable human will to rebuild and rise from the ashes, no matter the odds.

Grace under Fire - A SOAR Perspective

In the heart of a devastating crisis, amid the raging flames and the deafening chaos, Vikram Sharma stands as a beacon of leadership. His unwavering strength in the face of adversity is a testament to his character, a true embodiment of what it means to lead.

As he dons the fire-resistant suit and faces the inferno, Vikram's strength shines brilliantly. He coordinates rescue efforts, directs firefighting teams, and faces the media with composure. His decisiveness and determination are the pillars on which he builds his response to the disaster.

But amidst the relentless battle, Vikram also reveals a side often hidden in leaders of his stature—vulnerability. In the quiet moments, his eyes well with soot-streaked tears, and he questions his own role in the tragedy. He feels the weight of responsibility for his employees, their families, and the future of DynaGrow. His vulnerability makes him relatable, human, and deeply empathetic.

In this paradox, we find a powerful lesson for leadership. It's not about being strong or vulnerable; it's about seamlessly blending the two. True leadership lies in the ability to be strong when the situation demands it, to make tough decisions, and to lead by example. But it also lies in the courage to be vulnerable, to show empathy, and to acknowledge one's own limitations.

The essence of leadership is not in being flawless but in being real. It's in embracing the paradox of strength and vulnerability, knowing that they coexist to create a leader who inspires, empathizes, and, above all, leads with humanity. It's a lesson from the crucible of crisis that reminds us that leaders, like Vikram Sharma, are not superheroes but individuals who rise when needed, even as they acknowledge their own humanity.

Amidst the turmoil of a level 8 industrial disaster, Vikram Sharma's leadership journey unfolds as a captivating tapestry of strength and vulnerability, ambition and empathy, decisiveness and open-mindedness, vision and humility. As he faces the inferno, Vikram's strength shines brilliantly, and he stands as a beacon of leadership. His unwavering strength in the face of adversity is a testament to his character, a true embodiment of what it means to lead.

In the heart of the crisis, his first thought is to prioritize safety above all else. The safety of every individual involved becomes his unwavering mission. With strategic acumen, he assesses the disaster's scale and nature, crafting a tailored response to confront the unique challenges it presents.

Communication becomes his lifeline, and he wields it masterfully. Clear and empathetic, his words provide reassurance while managing expectations with realism. Vikram's decisions are swift and informed, but his adaptability shines through as he adjusts course with the evolving situation.

Leading by example, he remains a pillar of calm and composure amidst chaos, setting a standard of unwavering strength. His empathy, a source of solace to those affected, illuminates his path.

Resource allocation is meticulous, and collaboration is second nature. Vikram orchestrates resources efficiently and ensures seamless coordination with external organizations.

Throughout, Vikram's moral compass never wavers. Ethical considerations guide his decisions, and transparency is his beacon. Honesty, even in the face of adversity, forges trust.

Let's navigate these concepts through the SOAR model, offering simple steps that you can integrate into your daily leadership journey:

S - Self-Reflect

Take time each day to reflect on safety concerns in your workplace or personal life. Ask yourself, "What potential risks exist, and how can I mitigate them?" Keep a journal to track your safety reflections and improvements over time.

O - Own your Journey

Identify one area in your leadership role where you can set a better example. It could be maintaining composure during stressful situations or enhancing transparency in communication. Commit to improving in this area consistently.

A - Act with Persistence

Challenge yourself to make swift decisions in everyday situations. Practice weighing the pros and cons, trust your judgment, and act decisively. Gradually, this will become a habit that serves you well in moments of crisis.

R - Rise Higher

Set aside time to envision your organization's long-term goals and recovery strategies, even in times of stability. Create a plan for resilience and growth that encompasses your vision. Regularly revisit and revise this plan to adapt to changing circumstances.

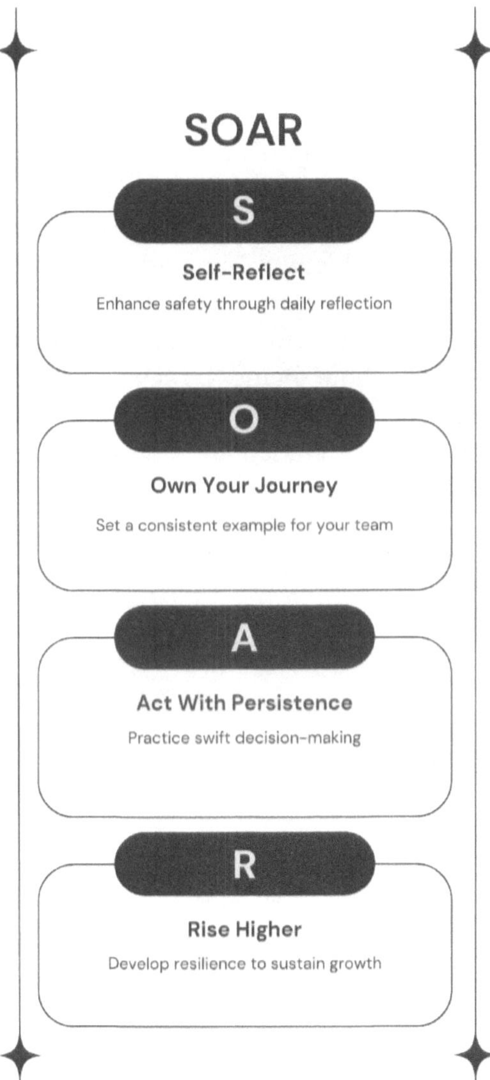
SOAR
S
Self-Reflect
Enhance safety through daily reflection
O
Own Your Journey
Set a consistent example for your team
A
Act With Persistence
Practice swift decision-making
R
Rise Higher
Develop resilience to sustain growth

These simple actions aligned with the SOAR model can help individuals develop and strengthen their leadership skills, fostering personal and professional growth.

The essence of leadership is not in being flawless but in being real. Vikram epitomizes the paradoxes of leadership, illustrating that true leaders navigate complexity with a blend of strength and vulnerability, ambition and empathy, decisiveness and open-mindedness, vision and humility. Remember that leadership isn't about being unwaveringly strong; it's about being strong when it matters, vulnerable when needed, and always guided by a vision tempered by humility.

Leading with Purpose

CHAPTER 6

Rising from the Ashes

In the aftermath of the devastating industrial disaster at DynaGrow, the ensuing months have unfolded as a harrowing journey. The company's financial foundation lay in ruins, its once-thriving operations had ground to a halt, and Vikram Sharma found himself navigating uncharted waters, grappling with challenges that threatened to engulf the very essence of the organization he had tirelessly built.

Vikram's initial priority was clear—rebuild and resurrect DynaGrow. He embarked on a Herculean quest to secure the essential resources and support required to pull DynaGrow back from the precipice. The fire that had mercilessly devoured their facility had also ravaged their finances, rendering the uphill battle ahead even more daunting. However, Vikram remains steadfast, resolutely refusing to yield to the clutches of despair.

During these darkest hours, a glimmer of hope emerges. Vikram and DynaGrow receive support from unexpected quarters. Industry peers and counterparts, who have long borne witness to Vikram's unwavering integrity and dedication, step forward in various capacities. Some offer much-needed financial assistance, while others provide their expertise and guidance. This collective outpouring of support serves as a lifeline during their time of dire need.

However, for Rajan, DynaGrow's path to recovery is marked by far greater complexity. The trauma of the fire, coupled with baseless accusations, weighs heavily on his shoulders. Malicious rumors, fanned by an individual with a vendetta, insinuate that the partners themselves are responsible for the fire, driven by dubious financial motives. The relentless media scrutiny and public backlash exact a heavy toll on Rajan.

The shock of witnessing his life's work reduced to ashes and the unjust blame heaped upon him by various sections of the media inflict deep wounds on Rajan's mental and emotional well-being. He withdraws into a shell, a mere shadow of his former self. The once-vibrant visionary has been replaced by a tormented soul, grappling to reconcile with the unfounded allegations that have tarnished his reputation.

While Rajan grapples with his inner demons, Vikram remains determined not to succumb to the prevailing darkness. He recognizes that the only viable path forward is to rebuild and reassert DynaGrow's legacy. The battle is relentless, with seemingly insurmountable odds, but Vikram is driven by an unwavering resolve to prove the naysayers wrong and restore DynaGrow to its former glory.

In the ensuing months, Vikram's leadership is subjected to the ultimate test. He navigates a treacherous course, fighting for financial stability, countering rumors, and, above all, safeguarding the integrity and reputation of DynaGrow. This is a battle that will not only determine their immediate future but also serve as a testament to the indomitable spirit of a leader who refuses to bow down to adversity.

Vikram is renowned for his unconventional ideas, and he doesn't disappoint this time either. One of these innovative ideas has arisen during his coaching discussions with Nirmala, where they have spent numerous occasions war-gaming crisis situations. Vikram proposes an ingenious approach to the clients—one that will not only maintain the supply chain but also reduce costs. Instead of reconstructing one massive unit similar to the one that has been reduced to ashes, he suggests creating several satellite units strategically located within or near the client's own plants.

The clients, along with their trusted industry peers, enthusiastically embrace Vikram's visionary proposal. They embark on a mission to scout locations and identify suitable spaces to establish these satellite manufacturing units. It is a collaborative effort driven by their shared belief in DynaGrow's resilience. The suppliers, acknowledging the need for logistical efficiency, also elevate their game to support this audacious endeavor.

This ambitious project sees Vikram crisscrossing the length and breadth of the country. It is a whirlwind endeavor, marked by long hours and relentless effort. Yet, Vikram remains undaunted, propelled by his unwavering commitment to DynaGrow and the unwavering belief that this innovative approach is the path to their recovery.

However, amid the flurry of activity, not all voices sing in harmony. Rajan, Vikram's closest partner and friend, finds himself at odds with Vikram's visionary concept. He struggles to see the merits of Vikram's plan, and skepticism clouds his judgment. A myriad of reasons why the satellite units are a perilous gamble swirl in Rajan's mind.

For Rajan, the idea of reconstructing the entire unit as it once was seems like the only viable path to recovery. He cannot bear the thought of enduring another setback. The scars of the disaster, both physical and emotional, run deep, and he believes that they cannot afford to take any more chances.

But Vikram, armed with his strategic acumen, knows that suspending the supply chain for the duration of a complete rebuild would be a risk they simply cannot afford to take. Their clients depend on them, and any disruption in supply could force these valuable clients to seek alternatives from competitors. The race to retain these crucial clients has already begun, and Vikram understands that losing ground is not an option.

In this moment of uncertainty and palpable tension, Vikram's leadership is once again put to the test. The choices he makes will determine not only the company's immediate future but also its long-term resilience and adaptability in the face of adversity.

Amid these challenges, Vikram's commitment to the company's recovery continues to shine brightly. He is not content with mere firefighting; he envisions DynaGrow's full recovery and a clear path forward. His unwavering dedication to learning from the crisis, identifying its root causes, and embracing improvement is steadfast.

Yet, not everyone within the DynaGrow family greets these developments with equal enthusiasm. Rajan, Vikram's closest confidant and the driving force behind DynaGrow's technical innovation, has seen his role diminish within the company even before the industrial disaster struck. The expansion into research and development (R&D) and the service business units has reshaped the company's dynamics, and Rajan has willingly withdrawn from the manufacturing side.

By the time of the accident, his involvement in manufacturing had become minimal, aligning with his preference for a reduced role in that area. However, the aftermath of the disaster has had a extreme impact on Rajan. He finds himself unable to concentrate on the R&D and Service units, which had previously been his domain.

Over the course of the two years dedicated to the company's recovery, these units have evolved to become largely self-sufficient, with Vikram overseeing them at the division heads' request. This transformation has not escaped Rajan's notice. His once-active involvement in these units has diminished, and he feels increasingly disconnected from the heart of DynaGrow's operations.

Rajan's withdrawal from active participation in the business is evident, and Vikram, perceptive as ever, notices the change. Yet, he chooses not to interfere, trusting that Rajan will overcome this challenging period in his own time. Moreover, Vikram's demanding responsibilities, which include overseeing the rebuilding of Unit-I and the management of Unit-II, leave him with limited capacity to address Rajan's evolving role within the company.

As internal tensions mount and the strain on their partnership becomes palpable, Vikram finds himself facing a delicate balancing act. He needs to navigate the shifting dynamics within DynaGrow, all while preserving the trust and friendship that have been the bedrock of their partnership. The challenge of leading DynaGrow through adversity is not only external but internal as well, as he seeks to maintain the delicate equilibrium that has defined their success for years.

Vikram's relentless efforts, fueled by his innovative approach, see DynaGrow's recovery taking shape at a remarkable pace. In just two short years, the company has managed to break even—a testament to Vikram's unwavering commitment and his ability to turn adversity into opportunity.

Amid the hustle and bustle of rebuilding and the complexities of managing multiple satellite units, a heartwarming surprise awaits Vikram. His family, an unlikely partner in the world of industrial challenges, steps up to stand beside him.

Priya, his steadfast wife, and their children, Diya and Jay, find themselves drawn into the heart of the crisis. They begin assisting Vikram in critical tasks, extending their support to duplicate his efforts across different satellite unit locations. It is a surprising turn of events for Vikram, who has never anticipated their keen interest in his work.

Together, they form a formidable core team, dedicated to the cause of resurrecting DynaGrow. Their dedication and enthusiasm are met with open arms by Vikram's teams back at work. The merging of both families into the DynaGrow family is remarkably seamless, a testament to the bonds forged through shared commitment and resilience.

Nevertheless, not all members of the DynaGrow family welcome these developments with equal enthusiasm. Rajan, Vikram's closest confidant, finds himself increasingly uneasy. The tensions have been simmering ever since Vikram overrode his rebuilding plans in favor of the satellite units.

Rajan can't shake the feeling that his role and influence within the company are diminishing. He has been the technical visionary, the driving force behind their innovation. But as Vikram's family becomes increasingly involved in critical decision-making and operations, Rajan feels marginalized.

The partnership that has once thrived on trust and shared vision now stands at a crossroads. The strain is palpable, and the future of their partnership hangs in the balance. It is a challenging time for Rajan, who grapples with his changing role and the shifting dynamics within DynaGrow.

In the face of these internal tensions, Vikram's leadership is once again put to the test. He needs to navigate the delicate balance between family and friendship, innovation and tradition, all while steering DynaGrow toward a brighter future.

The Crucible of Adversity: A SOAR Perspective

In the annals of leadership, where each decision carries the weight of destiny, there exists a paradox that we often grapple with — the delicate balance between decisiveness and open-mindedness. This paradox comes to life in the journey of Vikram, who faces their darkest hour.

DynaGrow, a symbol of innovation and resilience, is thrust into a crisis of unprecedented magnitude. A catastrophic industrial disaster has left the company's financial stability in ruins, and its operations lay in shambles. Vikram, a seasoned leader with a vision, finds himself at the helm of a sinking ship. The immediate choice is clear — rebuild.

Here, the paradox begins to unfold. Vikram's decisiveness comes to the forefront. He fights relentlessly, seeking the resources needed for DynaGrow's resurgence. The fire has scorched their finances, but it cannot incinerate his determination. He embodies the essence of decisiveness — the ability to make tough choices in the face of overwhelming odds.

Yet, Vikram's leadership is not a monolith of decisiveness. It bears the fingerprints of open-mindedness, a willingness to embrace unconventional solutions. In the darkness of despair, a unique proposition emerges. Vikram, known for his unconventional ideas, proposes the creation of satellite manufacturing units, a concept that blends supply chain continuity and cost reduction.

This is where the paradox deepens. Vikram's decisiveness is the driving force behind this audacious plan. He doesn't hesitate to present it to his clients, despite the skepticism it ignites. His unwavering belief in the idea is the mark of a decisive leader.

However, Vikram's open-mindedness plays a pivotal role. He seeks the collaboration of his clients and industry friends. He listens to their feedback, considers their input, and allows the idea to evolve. This willingness to adapt and innovate demonstrates open-mindedness in action.

The clash between decisiveness and open-mindedness manifests in the form of opposition from his closest confidant, Rajan. Vikram's decisiveness propels him to override Rajan's rebuilding plans in favor of the satellite units. The strain on their partnership is palpable, a testament to the paradoxical nature of leadership decisions.

Vikram's journey teaches us that leadership isn't about choosing one path over the other, but rather, it's about navigating the delicate dance between these paradoxes. Decisiveness without open-mindedness can lead to stubbornness, blind to the innovative ideas that may arise. Open-mindedness without decisiveness can result in a lack of direction, where opportunities slip through the cracks.

Let's navigate these concepts through the SOAR model, offering simple steps that you can integrate into your daily leadership journey:

S - Self-Reflect: Create a journal where you record your leadership decisions and the factors that influenced them. Regularly review and reflect on these entries to identify patterns and areas for improvement.

O - Own Your Journey: Seek feedback from colleagues and team members about your leadership style. Ask for specific examples where your decisiveness or open-mindedness had a positive or negative impact. Own both your strengths and areas for improvement.

A - Act with Persistence: Set a leadership goal for yourself, whether it's implementing a new strategy, fostering better team collaboration, or making a challenging decision. Commit to seeing this goal through, even when obstacles arise.

R - Rise Higher: Identify a leadership skill or trait you'd like to develop further, such as active listening, empathy, or strategic thinking complementing leadership your goal. Seek out resources, courses, or mentors that can help you rise higher in that particular aspect of leadership.

SOAR

S

Self-Reflect

Identify unique leadership patterns.

O

Own Your Journey

Seek feedback and embrace your strengths

A

Act With Persistence

Commit to your leadership goal

R

Rise Higher

Develop laser-focused leadership skills."

By aligning these actions with the SOAR model, you can work on your leadership skills in a structured and focused way, ultimately becoming a more effective and well-rounded leader.

Vikram Sharma, with his unwavering decisiveness and the wisdom to be open to alternative perspectives, exemplifies the art of balancing these paradoxes. His story illuminates the path for leaders who must make difficult decisions while remaining receptive to innovation and collaboration. It is a reminder that leadership is a paradoxical journey, where the ability to hold these opposing forces in harmony can shape destinies and lead organizations to brighter futures.

CHAPTER 7

Crossroads of Legacy

"Are you still with me, Vikram?"

The atmosphere in the boardroom, which had once borne witness to their unbreakable camaraderie, had now shifted, surrendering to a palpable tension. Rajan's question, tinged with an almost unrecognizable tone, sliced through the room's charged air, snapping Vikram back into the present. The inquiry didn't just echo in the room; it reverberated through the very fabric of their friendship. Trust, once a cornerstone of their partnership, now hung precariously in the balance.

Within a mere fraction of a second, Vikram experienced an epiphany—a crystalline understanding that their shared trials and triumphs had metamorphosed not just their venture, Dynagrow, but also their personal equations. The factory fire from years past had left its indelible imprint, not just on brick and mortar, but on flesh and blood.

The conversation had taken an acrimonious turn the moment Cho Seungri exited the room. A titan in global technology, Cho's presence had always commanded respect. Yet, to understand the layers beneath this tension, it's important to trace the origins of this relationship.

Years before the Daesan merger was ever on the table, Vikram had met Cho Seungri at a global technology summit in Tokyo. At that time, both were bright-eyed entrepreneurs, not yet the battle-hardened leaders they'd become. Their booths were next to each other, and despite representing competition, the air was never tense. Instead, it was filled with the smell of ink and ambition.

Cho was a unique figure, deeply imbued with a spirit of co-opetition—cooperation with one's competitors. His mentality was rooted in both traditional Korean business philosophy and modern-day Silicon Valley ethos. For Vikram, Cho was not just a competitor but a collaborator, a fellow visionary. Together, they had often pondered the nuances of emerging innovations even before they broke into public consciousness. This long-standing relationship and mutual respect were why Vikram was even considering this unprecedented merger.

For Vikram, Cho was a collaborator, a fellow visionary in the technological landscape. Together, they had often pondered over the nuances of emerging innovations, even before they broke into public consciousness.

Rajan, conversely, had always perceived Cho as a professional rival, pushing his team relentlessly to surpass the technological advancements heralded by Cho. Although his team had managed to keep pace, the years had dampened Rajan's competitive spirit, leaving him not quite the man he used to be.

The formal merger proposal that Cho tabled an hour prior had significantly rocked the boat but had not caught Vikram off-guard. In numerous subtle ways, he had been paving the way for this moment, preparing for this watershed occasion in consultation with Nirmala, his trusted confidante.

Rajan was disconcerted, feeling an acute sense of betrayal not only by the unexpected proposal but by Vikram's evident lack of surprise. It was as though a shadow of suspicion had once again been cast upon him, disrupting his mental equilibrium. The very notion of the merger proposal led Rajan to question not just their business partnership but also the emotional investment he had made in their friendship over the years.

Thus, this offer from Cho represented a crux—either a pivot towards reconciliation or a threshold that would propel them onto divergent trajectories.

The Rajan who had embarked on this journey was decidedly not the man who stood before Vikram now, a transformation that elicited a disconcerting sense of déjà vu in Vikram. It was reminiscent of a critical juncture from years ago when he had stood before the General Manager at the bank, deciding between a life of secure monotony and the uncharted realm of entrepreneurial adventure. The circumstances now were different, but the dilemma was eerily similar.

In the years since its inception, Dynagrow had transformed, becoming less of a venture and more of a sanctuary for Vikram—a realm that embodied his very identity. Now, he faced a question that gnawed at his soul: Was it time to say goodbye to this haven he had constructed, to embrace another grand adventure?

Both men had evolved, their trajectories now misaligned. Rajan and Vikram, once bound by a shared vision, had grown into disparate entities, each responsible for their own interpretive journey through the maze of successes and failures they had traversed.

Facing an unyielding ideological schism with Rajan and the stagnation of protracted negotiations, Vikram realized that the alternative he was considering had been years in the making. During the rebuilding phase of Dynagrow post the factory fire, Vikram had been meticulously observing Diya and Jay. It wasn't just casual paternal observation but a carefully calibrated assessment. He had involved them in strategic discussions, assigned them to lead smaller projects, and even had them shadow different departments—all with the intent of nurturing their nascent leadership capabilities. It was their subsequent successes and the mature poise they had displayed that formed the bedrock of his alternative proposal.

The nuances of this alternative were discussed during a private meeting with Cho at a secluded garden café. "You see, Cho, this isn't a spur-of-the-moment idea. Over the past several years, I've watched Diya and Jay not just grow but flourish, absorbing the ethos of Dynagrow while contributing to its fabric," Vikram shared, adding a personal touch to his professional rationale.

"I'd love for you to meet them, and sense the synergy for yourself."

Meanwhile, at home, Priya sensed a different air about her husband. "You look preoccupied," she observed. "Something with Cho?"

"We discussed an alternative path, a collaboration that could be a boon for everyone, including Diya and Jay," Vikram confided.

"How did he take it?" Priya asked.

"Cho is intrigued. But the real stake here is whether our children would be up for the challenge," he said, his eyes meeting Priya's, both aware of the weight of the pending decision.

Vikram felt it incumbent to consult with Rajan about the possible new direction involving Diya and Jay. They met in the same boardroom where so many pivotal decisions had been made. The atmosphere was noticeably different this time—somewhat subdued, but not as tense as it had been during their previous confrontation.

"Rajan, I have a proposal for the next phase of Dynagrow. I've been watching Diya and Jay closely over the years, particularly during our rebuilding period. They have shown remarkable aptitude, not just technically but in their grasp of sustainable business models. I have been in dialogue with Cho about a new tangent to Dynagrow's existing business. This doesn't intrude on your vision but complements it," Vikram laid out the plan carefully, watching Rajan for any signs of resistance.

Rajan looked up, his eyes meeting Vikram's, "You're saying this wouldn't affect the core of what we've built?"

"Exactly," Vikram affirmed, "It's an extension, one that could potentially open up new avenues without diluting what you and I have worked on so hard."

A discernible sigh of relief escaped Rajan's lips. "If it's a different pathway that I don't have to be directly involved in, I see no reason to oppose it. The truth is, I've been worried about what would happen once you stepped away. But if Diya and Jay can manage this new venture, it may actually be good for Dynagrow in the long run."

"Thank you, Rajan. This means a lot," Vikram felt a weight lift off his shoulders. It was as if the years of friendship, however strained, had reached a moment of reconciliation, if only briefly.

Vikram paused, carefully choosing his next words. "Rajan, after our last discussion, I've had a lot to reflect upon. I think it's time I step down from Dynagrow."

Rajan looked at Vikram, shock settling into his features. "Step down? Now? Just like that? After everything we've been through?"

Vikram nodded, a sense of sincerity in his eyes. "Yes, Rajan. I understand it's a drastic step, and I wouldn't make it without good reason. The tension between us has been building, and Cho's proposal pushed me to think hard about what's best for Dynagrow."

Rajan leaned forward, his brows furrowed. "But Vikram, we've had our share of disagreements over the years. Why does this one have to lead to you leaving?"

With a sigh, Vikram explained, "Rajan, it's not just about this one disagreement. It's about the overall direction we're heading in. Cho's proposal is logical, and I was inclined towards it, but it made me realize that our paths are starting to diverge significantly."

Rajan put up some resistance, his voice filled with concern. "Vikram, we've weathered so many storms together. Why break up the partnership now?"

Vikram met Rajan's gaze earnestly. "Rajan, our friendship is the most precious thing to me, and I don't want it to be marred by professional disagreements. This isn't the end, my friend, but a new beginning—for Dynagrow and for us."

After another hour of talking it out, Rajan leaned forward giving in to Vikram's decision. "So, what's the plan now?"

With a reassuring smile, Vikram explained, "I've already planned a process of restructuring. The idea is to make Dynagrow less dependent on individuals and more reliant on robust processes. Whether it's me, you, or anyone else leading, the company should thrive."

Rajan absorbed this with a mix of surprise and contemplation. "So, you mean even if you're not here, the company will keep going smoothly?"

"That's exactly what I mean," Vikram affirmed. "I want to leave behind a legacy that ensures Dynagrow's continued growth and stability, no matter who's at the helm."

Rajan sighed, with a bit of nostalgia. "You know, Vikram, I always thought we'd build and retire from this together."

Vikram's expression softened, and he said, "Our friendship, Rajan, should never be sacrificed for the sake of our professional journey. I see our paths diverging in a way that can actually strengthen Dynagrow and preserve what we've built over the years."

They exchanged a nod, their eyes locking in a shared understanding. It marked the end of an era, indeed. Rajan finally seemed to relent, his expression softening. "Alright, Vikram, if you truly believe this is the right move, I respect your decision. We've always found a way to make things work, and I trust we'll do the same this time."

Vikram smiled, gratitude in his eyes. "That's the Rajan I know."

When Vikram broached the subject with Diya and Jay, their initial response was one of humbled curiosity. "It's a significant responsibility, Dad. Are you sure we're ready?" Diya asked, the gravity of the proposal not lost on her.

"It's because I've observed your readiness over the years that I am confident about this. You've handled your leadership roles with such grace that I have every faith you'll not just fit but excel in these new roles," Vikram responded, his words enveloped in a quiet yet unmistakable air of assurance.

"With every challenge comes an opportunity for growth," Vikram gently reassured, "And I believe both of you have what it takes to steer this ship."

Parallel to this, Rajan found himself in a state of contemplation in his home office. He stared at the framed photo on his desk, a snapshot from their early days at Dynagrow. His brows furrowed as he mulled over the recent conversation with Vikram. It was as if a heavy cloud of uncertainty had settled over him, casting a shadow on his usually confident demeanor.

The mention of Cho's proposal had stirred a storm of conflicting thoughts within him. He had come to terms with the idea of collaborating with Vikram's children, recognizing the potential it held for Dynagrow's future. However, the prospect of Vikram leaving the company was an entirely different matter.

As he gazed at the photo, a sense of nostalgia washed over him. The memories of their journey from humble beginnings to the heights of success played like a montage in his mind. The thought of letting go of something they had built together was hard to fathom.

Despite his initial resistance, Rajan couldn't shake the feeling that Vikram's decision was too drastic. They had weathered countless storms together, and despite their differences, their partnership had always managed to steer the ship in the right direction. Rajan couldn't come to terms with the idea of forging ahead without his lifelong friend and partner.

As he continued to ponder, Rajan couldn't ignore the fact that Dynagrow had always been a testament to their adaptability and resilience. Maybe, just maybe, they could find a way to resolve their differences and continue their journey together, even if it meant some adjustments to their roles and visions for the company.

Cho was in town, and a dinner was planned at Vikram's residence, where Diya and Jay were to be formally introduced. For weeks prior, the siblings had been meticulously preparing a comprehensive presentation, integrating both technological foresight and sustainable business strategies. They knew that Cho was a titan in the industry, and they intended to match his expectations with their aspirations for Dynagrow.

As everyone gathered in the lavish living room after dinner, a projector was set up, and Diya and Jay began their presentation. Though tensions were high at first, the room was soon filled with the energy of intellectual engagement. Cho's questions were sharp, incisive, probing the depth of their understanding and foresight. Each query was met with well-articulated responses, and what started as a presentation evolved into an energetic discussion that covered various facets of technology and organizational growth.

As the clock hands swept past midnight and into the wee hours, it was evident that the trio had captivated Cho's attention. When they finally decided to call it a night, Cho turned to Vikram and confided, "Your children are extraordinarily prepared. They possess not just intelligence but also a rare kind of wisdom—the kind that's seasoned beyond their years, a quality seldom observed in emerging leaders today."

While Vikram's children were getting accustomed to their new roles, he couldn't help but reflect on a conversation with Nirmala a couple of months back. The topic had been hypothetical: "What would you do if Dynagrow was no longer part of your life?" Nirmala had asked. At that time, he had dismissed the notion but entertained her questions nonetheless. But he humored her, spinning tales of ventures that could pivot towards social change, stating that whatever he'd do, it would definitely involve leveraging his skills for a greater good. Looking back, Vikram realized that even then, he had subconsciously war-gamed a lot of pathways. As Vikram prepared for another transformative chapter, it occurred to him how prescient their conversation had been. The air was thick with the possibilities of things left unsaid, yet he felt an unprecedented clarity as though every step he had taken was leading to this very moment. Though he was stepping away from Dynagrow, Vikram knew that this was not the end, but merely a transitional portal to another compelling narrative, yet to be penned.

The Dance of Paradoxes: A SOAR Perspective

In the story of Vikram's remarkable journey, we find a rich fabric of leadership woven from the threads of intricate paradoxes. These paradoxes, when skillfully navigated, create the magical finesse of exceptional leadership. As we conclude this chapter in his life, we glean powerful lessons from his experiences, each lesson representing a vital aspect of effective leadership.

Strength and Vulnerability - A Delicate Balancing Act: Vikram's journey illustrates the intricate interplay between strength and vulnerability. His unwavering strength is the bedrock upon which he makes crucial decisions and ventures into uncharted territory. We witness this strength as he orchestrates transitions and explores new horizons, especially when he proposes the collaboration with Cho Seungri and introduces Diya and Jay as potential leaders. However, true leadership also demands vulnerability—the courage to address trust issues and the readiness to embrace change. Vikram's journey teaches us that strength and vulnerability are not opposing forces but complementary aspects of effective leadership, as he navigates the complexities of trust, change, and partnership.

Ambition and Empathy - The Heartbeat of Leadership: Driven by ambition, leaders like Vikram aspire to achieve greatness, innovate, and push the boundaries of success. Vikram's ambition is evident in his relentless pursuit of DynaGrow's success and his willingness to explore new opportunities, such as the collaboration with Cho Seungri. Yet, ambition must be tempered by empathy—a guiding force that compels leaders to consider the needs and aspirations of others. Vikram's empathy shines through as he recognizes not just the potential in Diya and Jay, but also Rajan's perspective of comforting stability. He refrains from pushing Rajan out of his tolerance zone at the same time finds ways of nurturing the growth of Diya and Jay, providing them with opportunities to lead. His story reminds us that ambition, when paired with empathy, can lead to meaningful and sustainable success, benefiting not only the leader but also the team and the organization.

Decisiveness and Open-mindedness - Navigating Uncertainty with Grace: Leaders must be decisive, capable of making tough choices even in the face of uncertainty. Vikram's decisiveness is evident in his proposals and strategic decisions, including the collaboration with Cho Seungri and the introduction of Diya and Jay as future leaders. However, decisive leaders must also be open-minded, receptive to new ideas and adaptable to change. Vikram's willingness to consider alternative solutions, especially when proposing the collaboration with Cho, demonstrates that decisiveness and open-mindedness can coexist harmoniously. His journey emphasizes that leaders who embrace diverse perspectives and remain open to change are better equipped to navigate challenges and seize opportunities in an ever-evolving landscape.

Vision and Humility - Crafting a Legacy of Service: In the final conversation between Rajan and Vikram, we witness a profound reflection of the paradox of Vision and Humility. This paradox is intricately woven into the fabric of their leadership journey, underscoring the complexity of their roles as leaders.

Vikram, as the visionary leader, exemplifies the element of Vision in this dialogue. He presents a forward-looking perspective, articulating his vision for DynaGrow's future. His visionary thinking is evident in his proposal for a new direction that involves Diya and Jay as potential leaders. Vikram's ambition to explore new horizons and create opportunities aligns with this facet of leadership. He recognizes the need to adapt and innovate, even if it means stepping aside from the helm, and his vision guides him in this path.

Conversely, Vikram's dialogue with Rajan also showcases Humility as a vital component of leadership. Despite his ambition and vision, Vikram humbly acknowledges that he may not be the future leader of DynaGrow. His humility is evident in his willingness to step down for the greater good of the company, emphasizing that leadership serves a purpose beyond personal achievement. His commitment to nurturing potential leaders, Diya and Jay, reflects a sense of humility, recognizing that the organization's success should be prioritized over individual aspirations.

Therefore, in this pivotal conversation, Vikram embodies the paradox of Vision and Humility. He illustrates how visionary leadership can coexist with humility, creating a harmonious balance that serves the organization's greater purpose. Vikram's journey serves as a testament to the intricate dance of leadership paradoxes, where strength and vulnerability, ambition and empathy, decisiveness and open-mindedness, and, in this case, vision and humility harmonize to orchestrate transformative change. As leaders, we are called to embrace these paradoxes, recognizing that exceptional leadership is a dynamic journey where these elements interplay, guiding us toward a brighter future, one paradox at a time. Vikram's story reminds us that leadership is not a destination but an ever-evolving tapestry of elements, and it is in their delicate balance that we uncover the true essence of leadership.

To put these lessons into action, consider the SOAR framework:

S - Self-Reflect on your Strength and Vulnerability:

Take time each week for self-reflection. Journal about a recent decision or challenge where you demonstrated strength and consider if vulnerability could have improved the outcome. Identify one aspect of vulnerability you can incorporate into your leadership approach.

O - Own your Journey of Ambition and Empathy:

Assess your ambitions and goals in a leadership context. Identify one goal or ambition and reflect on how it aligns with the needs and aspirations of your team or organization. Adjust your goal if necessary to better incorporate empathy into your leadership journey.

A - Act with Persistence using Decisiveness and Open-mindedness:

Practice decisiveness by setting a clear, achievable goal for your team. However, also act with persistence in staying open to feedback and adjusting your approach as needed. Commit to regular check-ins and adapt your strategy based on input from your team.

R - Rise Higher with Vision and Humility:

Develop a leadership vision for your team or organization. However, ensure this vision is grounded in humility by emphasizing the collective success rather than personal achievement. Share this vision with your team and ask for their input on how to achieve it together.

SOAR

S

Self-Reflect

Reflect on your inner strength and vulnerability in leadership

O

Own Your Journey

Harmonize ambition and empathy in your leadership journey.

A

Act With Persistence

Master the art of decisive yet open-minded leadership

R

Rise Higher

Elevate your vision with humility in leadership

In Vikram's intricate dance with leadership paradoxes, we discover a compelling narrative. His story serves as a testament to the art of leadership, where strength and vulnerability, ambition and empathy, decisiveness and open-mindedness, vision and humility harmonize to orchestrate transformative change. As leaders, we are called to embrace these paradoxes, for it is in their delicate balance that we uncover the true essence of leadership—an ability to inspire, adapt, and pave the way for a brighter future, one paradox at a time. Vikram's journey reminds us that exceptional leadership is a journey, not a destination, and the tapestry of leadership is ever-evolving.

www.ingramcontent.com/pod-product-compliance
Lightning Source LLC
Chambersburg PA
CBHW021551150726
47990CB00006B/2496